SEXY & CONFIDENT
HOW TO BE THE DREAMGIRL MEN WANT, HAVE A BETTER LIFE AND IMPROVE YOUR SELF-ESTEEM

SEXY & CONFIDENT

How To Be The Dreamgirl Men Want, Have a Better Life and Improve Your Self-Esteem

ASH GREEN

ARTRUM MEDIA

For the girls who know they deserve more from life.

CONTENTS

HELLO, DREAMGIRL

This book is written with the sole purpose of motivating you.

I want to motivate you to do everything in your life better than the way you're doing it now. I want you to date better. I want you to think more highly of yourself. I want you to be more confident. It doesn't matter what you do or how you're doing it, even it you're doing it excellently, I want you to do it better. Everyone is capable of more. This is especially true of how you view yourself and how you are perceived. You are no exception.

Regardless of how she views herself, every woman wants to be sexy and confident. She wants to be the type of girl that is both sure of herself but is also wanted by men. She wants men to want her for herself and not because she has to lower herself in order to get their attention. She also wants to be taken seriously in the workplace and in life. The problem is that most women think that lowering themselves is the only way to succeed in life. They think that they have to be something they aren't in order to fit in and accomplish their goals. They either think they have to act like a bitch to get ahead in business or act like a complete ditz in order to get men to notice them. Trying to fit into these stereotypes just makes being a woman so much harder than it should be.

While both of these viewpoints will work, are they really necessary? Isn't there a middle ground where a woman can be both attractive and competent? Isn't there a middle ground where a woman can just be herself? Where she can both be hardnosed but still feminine? I say that there is. This middle ground is what it means to be sexy and confident. This is what it means to be true to yourself and everything that you can be in life. It's about bringing out the best in yourself as a woman while still being a woman. And let me tell, you a woman who can achieve both of these qualities will be a dreamgirl not only to the men in her life but also to herself. This is because she will be able to achieve everything that she has ever dreamed possible.

Women have so much to offer and by all rights should have the advantage over men in almost every situation. Women have what men want. Women *are* what men want. The only problem is that women undermine themselves by either trying to act like the guys in situations where guys dominate or they tear each other down in situations that are their own domain. They never give themselves the opportunity to use their unique gifts they have just by virtue of being female. As a result, they often end up feeling *less than*, dating bad men or just losing out on everything they could have achieved otherwise. This is why you have to find the balance between ballbreaker and heartbreaker, between a hard nose and a powdered one.

So sexy and confident? Of course. Dreamgirl? It's a given. You just have to figure out the balance that will work for you. It's possible for every woman to be the best that she can. In fact it's her right as a woman. All it takes is figuring out what she needs to enhance and what she needs to minimize. After all, women are promised their Prince Charming from childhood and since he doesn't exist, there needs to be something that compensates for his absence. This means having the life and self-esteem you deserve. No two people are the same, but the end result is. How you get there is up to you, but I am going to give you some tips on what you can do to help you achieve the desired result. You also need to realize that it doesn't matter what you do professionally. Whether you're a waitress or an attorney, you are capable of being the best you that you can be. It doesn't matter what you do when you are sexy and confident. You always have something to bring to the table in any relationship and any situation. And that something is *yourself.* And that's all you need.

So bye-bye, old you and hello, dream girl. It's time to become sexy and confident.

YOU'RE WORTH IT

You're worth it.

Yes, you have value and you're worth every bit of effort that it will take to make you feel better about yourself. It doesn't matter how badly you feel about yourself or how others have treated you. Whatever has happened to you in your life or whatever mistakes you've made are irrelevant. You deserve better. You're worth the effort to make yourself better and you're worth every good thing that happens to you as a result. Despite what others may say to you or how hard they might try to tear you down. It doesn't matter if they think improving yourself is a complete waste of time, you're worth it. And because of the fact that you're worth it, you should also know that you deserve better than what you've been getting.

Yes, you deserve better. You deserve a good life. You deserve a good job and you deserve a good man. You deserve everything that every other woman who has it together has. You're no different. So what if you haven't had the right breaks or the right luck? Just because you might not have had any of these things up to now means nothing. All it means is that you haven't had them yet and that the best is yet to come. Or course, there are some people who will say that you don't deserve anything in life and that thinking this gives you a false sense of entitlement. They subscribe to the "life is misery" idea and think that luck or merely hard work are the only determinants in having a good life. However, if you look at the people who say this, most of the time, they're doing pretty well for themselves. They're married and/or successful. It almost seems that they want to elevate themselves by comparing themselves to people who have not achieved this same level of success yet. This is just a little pathetic and completely unnecessary. While I think there is some truth to the fact that luck and hard work are important, I think that everybody deserves a good life and it is within reach. This is especially true if one goes about it the right way and has a good attitude.

When people try to tear you down and say that you're just wasting your time trying to improve yourself, you have to remember that they are coming from a place of negativity. They don't want you to succeed because it will either diminish what they have if they are successful or they will look bad because they didn't have the initiative to do better themselves. You can't listen to these people. If possible, surround yourself with positive people who aren't going to tear you down. Just because some negative bitter person thinks that they themselves are beyond improving, doesn't mean that you aren't. As long as you know that you can do better, you will do better. And believe me, everyone can do better. Even if they're already doing well.

So much of the time, women keep themselves from truly experiencing and enjoying the good things that life has to offer because they either think that they aren't good enough or don't deserve it. They may also think they're being selfish and want too much for themselves when so many other people aren't doing that well. In any case, this is where they are wrong. They find themselves in bad relationships with men and other people simply because they think that there's no alternative. They just need to know that a good life is out there for the taking if they just get out of their own way and let themselves experience it. Many women are their own worst enemies. When they think like this, this is especially true. Sabotaging yourself, regardless of the reason, is not going to help anyone. Most of the time, however, they don't even know they're doing this. They think that this is simply the way things ought to be. They know no other way.

Well, there is. If you just wake up and understand just what is going on around you, you will realize where you might be going wrong. A little bit of enlightenment can go a long way and if you get a full view of the problem, you can usually fix it easily. Just because bad things and bad people have happened to you in the past is no reason for them to keep happening. Each day is a new day and if you can just bring yourself to the point where you start to expect good things to happen to you, they will start happening for you. If you can just start realizing that you are above and beyond all the baggage that weighs you down, then you will rise above it.

You are good enough and you deserve better. The only person stopping you is yourself. If you can just raise your expectations, then you will begin to see the wonderful things that life has to offer. This is the secret of being sexy and confident and moreover, this is the secret to a happy life. You know that you deserve better and that you're worth it. You know that when bad things happen to you, it's not because you deserve it, it's just because they happened. This is just the way it is sometimes and is no indicator that they will continue to be this way. You're only doomed to a bad life if you keep doing the same things that made you have a bad life in the first place. There's no one saying that you have to keep doing them. You can take a different route and change. You have to keep in mind that good things happen too and that they will happen to you. You deserve it.

The upshot is that if you want to be a sexy and confident woman, you have to realize that you are a woman who deserves better and will expect no less. This doesn't make you egotistical, it just makes you a person who isn't willing to let the world or bad people push you around any more. You have to realize that you are worth every good thing that can happen to you. You deserve every good thing that life has to offer. You have to realize that you are only as good as you allow yourself to be and if you pull out the stops, then you can be as great as you want.

SEXY? AND CONFIDENT?

In an ideal world, it wouldn't matter so much how people present themselves. If a woman wanted to fully and openly display her sexuality then there would be no problem. She could do as she liked and flaunt her every asset whereever or however she pleased. Or, if she was the complete opposite in regards to her sexuality, she could be as buttoned up as she wanted without anyone calling her uptight or priggish. It just wouldn't matter. However, we don't live in an ideal world and neither one of these scenarios is completely feasible. We live in the real world and in the real world, presentation is everything. How you comport yourself will make or break you. If you're too open and too sexual, you'll be looked at as a slut. If you're too conservative, you're mousy and timid. In the real world, you're usually one thing or the other in regards to almost everything. Many people want to define you in some way and will use whatever you give them against you. It's a very fine line between slutty and sexy as well as between modest and timid and this can really cause today's woman a lot of problems in trying to find her place without seeming too much of one thing or another.

It's true. To most women, how she is perceived is everything. Are men attracted to her? Do other women respect her? Do men respect her? And most importantly, does she respect herself? Is she taken seriously? Do people think she's a bubblehead? Do they think she's a ballbreaker? These are all the questions that come up in regards to how a woman is viewed. That's why it's important to strike a balance between the most common elements by which most people judge women. These elements just happen to be appearance and attitude. Most people judge a woman on how she looks and how she acts. All other attributes are secondary and if a woman is to be taken seriously by both men and women, in the workplace and the dating world, she has to look and act her best. She has to live in two worlds. A woman who is sexy and confident is bridging both these worlds and these two attributes complement each other perfectly. Her confidence makes her sexy and her sexiness adds to her confidence. She knows that she is indeed someone special and would make an excellent girlfriend or wife, but is perfectly capable of standing on her own two feet in the workplace.

So what exactly does sexy and confident mean? It means that a woman can show the world that she is a sexy and desirable person yet still exude the confidence that shows that she's capable of handling herself in any situation. Sexy might mean showing a little bit of leg or maybe revealing a little cleavage, but with the aura that gives people the impression that while this may be one attractive girl, she is definitely the one that can get the job done. Sexy and confident means being comfortable in your skin as both a woman and a human being. A sexy and confident woman gets things done because she puts people at ease. She's being herself and is confident to know what she wants and is sexy enough to make people not forget that she is a woman.

One of the problems that many women have is that they think that they cannot be both sexy and confident. They think that if they are too confident, men will think that they are a bitch and if they are too sexy, then other women will think that they are sluts. As a result they try to compensate. They wear unflattering clothing to keep the women at bay or they act like ballbreakers to beat the men at their own game. Or they take the complete opposite route and slut it up to charm the men and are subsequently hated by the women. Regardless, these women aren't true to their femininity or themselves and are usually unhappy. This kind of behavior is not well-suited for anyone and is usually the result of a low self-esteem. This is just a way of catering to the lowest common denominator and will always ultimately leaving you feeling just a little less than what you are capable of being. Besides, it's impossible to win in this situation anyway. If you're not true to yourself, you will not please anyone and certainly not yourself. You have to be the best you can be. If you dumb yourself down for a man, then women will not respect you and if you act like you're beaten down around other women, men will just think you're weak.

So the next time you even entertain a doubt about being sexy and confident, just remember that if you can achieve this balance, the world will be yours. You just have to be yourself and do everything you can to be the best you can be. If you try to be less than who you really are by either catering to what you think other men or women want, you're just cheating yourself and will ultimately lose in the end. The world belongs to a sexy and confident woman because people find her attractive and smart. If a woman does not try to be all she can be, she is only cheating herself.

WHAT MEN WANT

Many women drive themselves crazy trying to figure out what men want. They look at movies and television and also real life and try to come up with a plausible answer. Do men want bimbos? Do they want smart women? Do they want tomboys? Just what do they want? As a result of this kind of thinking, women also drive themselves crazy trying to be what they think men want and trying to give men what they think men want. As a result, they usually change themselves for the worse and wind acting like a person completely unlike the person they really are. It's no better than when the smart kid dumbs down in school so she'll be accepted by all the less intelligent children. It can be actually a little embarrassing to see a woman who is trying to do this. This is because ultimately the man she is trying to please will use her and then walk over her on his way out the door.

You don't have to be like this. In fact, a sexy and confident woman would never lower herself to please a man because by being sexy and confident, she is in effect pleasing to all men. A sexy woman never has to have anyone validate her. She does not need anyone's approval because she loves herself and is not trying to do anything specifically to please a man. This is because she knows what men want. At least out of her. She knows that men want her to be herself—at least the men worth having. She knows that the right man will like who she is and she will not have to change to suit him. She knows that a man worth having will want her for who she is and not what she has to give him—or do for him.

A woman who is trying to please a man is very easily used. This happens in many different ways too—sexually and also monetarily. This is because when she is trying to please, she is vulnerable emotionally. I've seen it over and over again, women who try to buy men's affections. They will get pregnant to keep these men and even commit crimes for them only to ultimately be rejected. This is because these men aren't worth having. A man worth having can't be bought with things and he can't be bribed by anything other than a woman's affections. Men who have to be treated like this are already on their way out the door. They're just staying around long enough to get what they can out of a woman.

So what do men want? The question should be: *What do men worth having want?* The answer is *you*. The right one will want you and nothing else. He will accept you with all your flaws as well as your good points. If you find yourself having to open your checkbook to please a man, run. This man isn't interested in you. He's interested in what he can get out of you. There's a big difference. Sure, you should do everything in your power to improve yourself, but you should never change who you are, the person who is begging to be freed from the cage of self-doubt and low self-esteem that you've created for yourself.

The bottom line is that good men want the same thing as women do. They want good relationships with good women like you. If they want anything other than that, they don't want you. Move on.

REINVENT YOURSELF

For a moment, pretend you're a chef. And not just any chef, a great one. You know that there's a particular dish that you would like to prepare. You know exactly what it is and how it is supposed to look and taste. From this information, you can conceptualize what it's going to take to make this dish. You know what ingredients you need in order to accomplish the end result. Unless you're purely experimenting, you don't go blindly into it. And even if you are experimenting, you should have some idea of what it is that you're going to prepare. Otherwise, you end up with something completely different from what you were aiming for. Most of the time, this is not the desired outcome.

When you decide to become sexy and confident, this scenario is very similar to what you're going to have to do. You're going to have to visualize what exactly it is that you want to become and then work on what it takes to become it. This doesn't mean that you're going to have to change who you are at your core, but you will have to change how you approach life. If you want to be a sexy and confident woman, you're going to have to reinvent yourself. You're going to have to change the old you into the new you. How much this involves is up to you, but you have to come to grips that you will have to make some changes.

So, how do you do it?

As I said earlier, you need to visualize what exactly it is that you're trying to accomplish. What kind of sexy and confident woman is it that you want to become? You need to look at yourself and see what exactly it is that you need to add to accomplish this. Do you need to gain confidence? Do you need to be a little sexier? Do you need to be less brash? In the beginning you will need to look at yourself and figure out your weaker points. Try to determine where you need improvement. Are you timid? Are you easily intimidated by men? By other women? Whatever it is, take note. This is what you need to improve. And on this same note, you will also have to look at things about yourself that you may need to eliminate or tone down. Just keep in mind your desired result and then work towards it. Add and subtract whatever you need to in order to get there. Remember that you're not necessarily trying to change who you are, but rather you are trying to *improve* who you are. You are probably already a pretty cool person, but you may have some stuff you just need to tweak a little.

You may, in some drastic circumstances, have to take a long hard look at your friends. Are they what's bringing you down? Does being around them cause you to be more likely to engage in behaviors that you would rather not engage in? If so, you might want to think about hanging around a different group of people.

One of the key things you need to remember is that most of the things that are weighing you down are easy to overcome if you can only recognize that they exist. Most people go through life doing the same stupid things or acting the same way simply because they never question why they do these things. They just automatically do them. This is why you need to take stock of the things that are making you be less than you want to be. After that you need to consciously make an effort to overcome these bad behaviors.

Most of the time timidity and bashfulness, along with dowdiness and frumpiness, are simply a habit. The same thing goes with being brassy or obnoxious. Sure, some people are more prone to this kind of behavior than others, but at any rate, how you act towards others can be improved. Make a conscious effort to stop whatever it is that you're doing wrong and try to do better. If you're timid, be bold. If you're mousy, make yourself known. If you make the effort long enough, pretty soon it will be easy to put yourself out there as a more confident woman. Remember, you're trying to improve yourself. This is what you need to keep in mind.

Another thing you can do is to model better behavior. That is to say, fake it until you make it. If you pretend to be a confident person long enough, pretty soon, you will find that this behavior is sticking and you will become more confident. I heard a story of a criminal who had reformed his behavior. When asked how he did it, he said that he simply pretended to be a good person. This is what sustained him. And after a period of time of doing this, he found that he was a good person. He had been completely reformed. He wanted to do better with his life so he did the only thing he knew to do and that was to con himself into it and it worked.

The same thing applies to your confidence and your sexiness. If you're unsure of how a sexy and confident woman acts, look around you and find one and observe her behavior. She can be a movie actress, a movie character, a character from a book or even someone you know. Regardless, look at the woman and see what it is that makes her confident. How does she carry herself? How does she act around men and other women? Figure it out and try to emulate the behavior you admire. You'll find soon enough that you are changing your bad habits and picking up good ones.

Improvement will take time and effort, but it is not impossible. If you can just realize that you will have to make changes to be a sexy and confident woman, it will be that much easier to *become* a sexy and confident woman. Just realize that no one is perfect and that we all can stand for some improvement. Just don't be too hard on yourself when you're evaluating the stuff you need to change. You're probably already a great person; you just need to work on the stuff that needs improvement.

YOUR PAST MEANS NOTHING

Everyone deserves a better life and a fresh start. People make mistakes and have missteps. This is life. No one should keep you from becoming the person that you want to be. This means that in spite of what you may have done or what image you may have displayed before, your past means nothing. Today is a new day.

What this means is that there is still hope for you whether you have previously put yourself out there as being a bubble-headed Barbie doll or if you've presented yourself as being an asexual wallflower. You can reinvent yourself. It also means that even if you were a complete slut and would do anything just to get a man's attention you can still turn things around.

But it can only happen if you take steps to improve yourself. You have to change these bad behaviors. You have to evolve. You have to change slutty into sexy. You have to change timid into confident. You have to make the effort. If you don't, you're just going to keep doing the same stuff over and over again and no one will accept the new you because there will be no new you to accept.

After you take the steps to improve, you will have to present the new you to the public. This will be very tough because it will seem like you're almost a different person, but keep in mind that you're evolving. Over time, people will soon accept the new you and will forget the old one.

You just have to make the effort. For example, think about when you last changed your hairstyle. At first everyone commented on it, but eventually they soon forgot the old one. The thing to remember is that most people's minds are not filled with images of you. Outside of those in your immediate family, they probably don't even think of you that much. There's a saying about people who think that other people are constantly thinking of them are surprised to find out that they rarely are. This is why you must use this to your advantage. This is why it's okay to change.

So what if you used to be a little promiscuous? So what if you're thought of as one of the boys? So what? Don't be afraid to change. Sure, you may feel a little foolish when you start to change, but the more confident and sexy you start to feel, the more foolish you'll feel about how you used to be. Just look at it this way—do you really want to be stuck in your old way of life because of fear? Sometimes moving forward means that you must forgive yourself for your past bad behavior. You may have to admit to yourself that you used to take the wrong approach to life. This is okay. Move on. You're human. You were probably only doing the best you knew how to do at the time. The thing is that you know differently now. You know better now and you're doing better. Don't live in the past. Sometimes it means letting it all go and realizing that today truly is a new day.

Sure, there are going to be some people who will not accept the new you. To not realize this is to not be realistic. Some people simply will not accept or tolerate change in anything or anybody. They like their worlds to stay static. They want things to always remain the same. You need to ignore these people and continue about your improvement. You will never impress these people and you don't need to base your life around pleasing them. Remember you need to do what will work to improve *you*. Trying to please the unpleasable will not improve anyone. In fact, it's probably part of why you've been afraid to improve yourself up until now.

So, remember your past means nothing. The future is what's important. Never be afraid to look like a fool if it means improving yourself. Never be afraid to do better. Never be afraid of what people will say about your attempts to be a better person. Don't let anyone rain on your sexy and confident parade of self-improvement. The only opinion that matters is yours. You're the one who has to live with yourself. And if you're happy with yourself and the advances you've made, then that's all that matters. You just need to realize that most people will be happy for you and will be glad that you're doing better. It will be tough to make those first steps, but just make them. After you get started, you'll gain momentum and it will get easier. Sure, people may comment at first, but just be assured, in a very short while, their only impression will be of the new you.

CONFIDENT, BUT NOT BITCHY

Every assertive, self-assured woman has faced this problem.

If she dares to stand up for herself, assert her opinion or just hold her ground, she is referred to as a bitch. She is said to be a ballbuster. A hardass. Fact of the matter is that sometimes this may be true. But it doesn't have to be. There are always better ways to communicate. That is, if you can learn to do it in the right way.

It's true that most people mistake the confident woman as being a bitch. The type that emasculates men and then serves up their balls for lunch. Actually there's a lot of truth to this. Many confident women are this way. But it isn't their fault. They are this way because they *have* to be this way otherwise they will get chewed up in the business world.

But the sexy and confident woman is different.

She can be a ballbuster, but she isn't. She can be as rough and tough as the men but she doesn't have to be. In other words, this is because knows that she can use her femininity to get things done. She doesn't have to out-masculine the men because she's not a man and to do so would not really come off that well.

Women and men are diferent. A sexy and confident woman takes this information to heart and uses it to her advantage. She knows that as a woman she will have certain advantages over men. She uses this in everything. In matters of relationships, her confidence guides her. In matters of business, it's a combination of the two qualities. Regardless, she knows what she wants and doesn't let insecurity stop her.

One of the biggest obstacles that many women have when they want to assert their confidence is the fear of being perceived as being bitchy. They don't want everyone to think that they're either some heartless ballbreaker or some unhappy broad who is so miserable in her own life that she has to ruin everybody else's.

I'm sure you know some of these women hence you know exactly what I'm talking about.

Well, don't worry. This is not really a problem. The reason why is because confidence has nothing to do with bitchiness. It has to do with being comfortable in yourself to know when you're right and being big enough to admit when you're wrong. The confident woman is smart enough to know that she's still right even when she's wrong if she only admits to it and does better next time.

Many women and girls get the idea that the key to being perceived as confident is to steamroll or berate everyone around them until they get their way. However, while this may sometimes be somewhat effective as far as results go, it is usually more indicative of a person who lacks confidence rather than a person who has it. They are like a bullfrog who tries to puff himself up to be as big as he can possibly be in order scare off predators. Sometimes it works. Sometimes it doesn't. However, it doesn't really make him any stronger within. It just makes him look stronger. A confident person doesn't have to do this. Look at confident, effective men if you want an example. Notice how they usually don't have to run over everyone to get what they want. They simply know what they want and expect it out of life. They don't have to bully anyone into anything because it's unnecessary. They exude confidence which is then picked up on by the other people around them. As a result of this, people trust their judgement and opinion and usually do as they request. What they want out of people makes sense. They don't have to berate people into seeing it because they already know that they must know what they're talking about. Use this as your example.

You have to realize is that a lot of the time, coming off bitchy instead of confident is usually just a habit. It's something you probably learned from the women in your life when you were growing up. If you have a problem with confidence, it's highly probable that either your mother yelled and screamed to get her way with the kids and your dad or she was quiet and timid and always deferred to your father for everything. If you are actually a confident person, then your mother probably was also confident. Or your father. These sorts of behaviors are learned. This is why you have to make improvements and learn new ones if you are going to be a sexy and confident woman.

The same thing goes for your relationships as it does in the office. You will be perceived as much more confident if you're nice and expect the best out of people rather than you try to berate them into doing what you want. You've heard the old saying about how you attract more flies with honey than vinegar? This is exactly what confidence is about. When you're confident, you can get what you want without trying too hard and be better liked in the process. Sure, there may be times when you'll have to assert yourself. This may be a little tough, but if you've got faith in your convictions and stand your ground and do it in as nice a way as possible, then you'll accomplish great things.

You have to find the balance between confidence and bitchiness. You will have to do this by taking stock. Look at people who are bitchy or timid. Do you do some of the same things that they do? Do you act like them in particular situations? When you ask someone to do something are you afraid that if you don't yell at them, they won't do it? Apply this to all aspects of your life. Just understand that if you know what you want and know that you deserve it, you can usually get it if you're nice, firm and persistant. Just be yourself and don't be so scared that you have to resort to steamrolling or shying away. After all, both behaviors are, in essence, merely indicative of the same thing.

And how do you become confident without being bitchy? It's easy. All you have to do is to assert yourself with finesse. Once you decide that you need to do something or that you need to stand your ground or whatever, you stand your ground in a nice way. You have to be like a velvet hammer. You are tough, but you are also feminine. You use your assets to your advantage, but you do not let anyone take advantage of you and you do not get intimidated. Most people will back down when they see that you will push back and not be ignored. You just have to stand your ground until they do. And if they won't? This is where finesse comes in. You stand your ground, but try to find a way to do this so that everyone can leave happy. Most people will give a little if they feel like they're getting something in return.

So the name of the game when it comes to getting your way without being considered a bitch is to be strong, know what you want and demand that you get it. You don't have to yell and scream to do it, you just have to use your wits and keep your cool. This is the way that confident people operate.

You can do this! Just be the best you that you can be and you'll be okay. If you have to model confidence in the beginning, it's okay. Just so long as you start improving yourself. Once you start, you'll soon see vast improvements in the way you act towards other people and how they act towards you. You will gain momentum and pretty soon you'll find that you can get most everything you want and will be able to accomplish great things in both your professional and personal lives. And you'll do this without being a bitch.

HISTORY REPEATING?

Do you ever feel that you're cursed when it comes to love?

Yes, cursed?

Consider this for a moment: Do you ever wonder why the same bad stuff seems to keep happening to the same people over and over again? Have you wondered why some people just seem to be jinxed?

Using the same train of thought, have you ever wondered why you find yourself in bad relationships? Have you ever wondered why you keep falling for the same kinds of men who are inevitably always wrong for you? Over and over again? And you're convinced that no matter how sexy or confident you become, you're doomed to a life of dating and relationship turmoil.

Of course, your first thought would indeed be that you're cursed, or that there's something wrong with you. Is it really the fact that you keep meeting the same kind of men? Or is it because you think that it's just the way things are? That you're just unlucky in love?

Probably the answer lies in all of these. But it also may be because it's all you know. This is just how you think that relationships should be. You have simply been brought up to think that this is the way that things should be between two people who are dating. You think that harmony is a just something that you hear in your favorite music, not something that should happen in a relationship.

Before you discount what I'm saying, you need to ask yourself the following questions: Was there a lot of conflict in your house when you were growing up? Did you parents always argue? How about you and your siblings? Were you always fighting with each other? If this is the case, is it any wonder that you have so much conflict in your adult relationships? It's what you know. It's *all* you know, in other words. And if this all you know, then how are you expected to imagine anything else? You shouldn't beat yourself up over this, either. Just take note and realize that people do get along. People in a relationship are capable of treating each other well. Just because you haven't seen it for yourself, don't think that it doesn't exist. You deserve to be happy in a relationship—even though everyone you have seen in one isn't.

So what can you do about it? This is easy. As I just said, recognizing this situation is the important thing. If you can recognize that's this is what is going on in your life and that you have only been exposed to negative relationships, you can actively make changes to fix it.

Do you find yourself bullying and badgering the men you date? Ask yourself if this is how your mother treated your father. Or is the other way around? Do men bully and badger you? Maybe the same dynamic existed in your family but in reverse. The saying about people who don't know their history are doomed to repeat it is very true. However, when it comes to dating and relationships, it's that people who don't recognize how their past is affecting their present are doomed to the same heartaches over and over again in the future. If you can just recognize how your childhood relationships can affect how you view your adult relationships, you can start to make positive effective changes. Whether this means changing how you act or by simply dating better men or not putting up with bad behavior is up to your particular situation. You just have to see it and if something is ringing true, do something about it.

So look back and see the patterns. Do you see anything familiar? If you do, then there's no better time than now to start fixing it. How you do this is to just be conscious of this and then try to break the pattern. If you're just aware of how your past is affecting your future, it should be fairly easy to make positive changes to how you're doing things. Once you do this, you will soon start to change into a much more confident and self-assured woman. You have to always keep in mind that you deserve happiness. It doesn't matter what has happened in your life before now. It doesn't matter if no one you know has ever experienced a happy relationship. It just doesn't matter about this stuff. What matters is that you recognize that you've been brought up with low expectations and the sooner you start raising them and expecting happiness, the sooner you'll get it.

INDEPENDENT BUT NOT ISOLATED

The crazy cat lady.

You know her. She's the perpetually single woman who is alone in life except for her cat—or cats. She eats alone. She shops alone and she sleeps alone. That is, except for the cat. Do you think that she just ended up this way by chance? Do you think that she wanted to become like this? No, she didn't. She probably started out just like everybody else, except for one thing. She decided that she wanted to go it alone. She wanted to go it alone despite the consequences. She probably considered herself to be fiercely independent. She could do everything herself and she didn't need some man to help her. The problem is that she couldn't see far enough in the future to glimpse just where this would lead.

The one problem that many women who want to be sexy and confident make is that they mistake the concept of independence with the idea that they must "go it alone" in life. They think that they must be on the outside, always doing for themselves, always putting out that "strong" image. Somewhere along the line, this attitude usually leads to them separating themselves from the world. They begin to think that everyone who needs someone else is weak. They will show the world. They are women who need no one. They are islands. They are invincible.

Sadly though, many women who think like this ultimately live lives filled with cats, broken appliances and empty social calendars. These women fail to recognize that they are turning their independence into isolation. They get so hung up on the idea that they *need* no one that they forget that they may actually *want* someone with whom to share their lives. They push away everyone in an attempt to show just how much they don't need to depend on anyone. While in the beginning of a woman's journey for self-sufficiency this may be looked at as plucky, in the end it just looks a little sad.

You have to learn that being strong has nothing to do with being alone. It is far harder to make a relationship work than it is to be by yourself. By yourself, you can do anything. You are the mistress of your domain. However, while this may be fun at first, how fun is it once you find it hard to turn back the tide of isolation? You have to know that you can be strong and be in a relationship, too. So many people have been fooled into thinking that they're strong simply because they take the path less traveled. It's less traveled for a reason when it comes to this subject. If one relationship doesn't work out, then move on to the next one. Don't let a bad relationship be your life changing event. Don't let it be the catalyst in your transformation into the crazy cat lady.

A sexy and confident woman may be independent but she knows that as a human being she needs the company and companionship of other people. She knows that while she's perfectly capable of changing the oil in her vehicle (or paying someone else to do so), she also doesn't resist it when a man, maybe one that likes her, offers to do it for her. It's about achieving a balance. Just because you can do everything on your own, like going on vacation, buying a car, going shopping or whatever, do you really want to? Especially if it's only to make a point that you are independent? Loosen up. A sexy and confident woman is not looking for validation. She's fine on her own. However, this doesn't mean that she has to go to great lengths to prove her independence or strength. She simply is independent and strong. She is confident in that. As I keep saying, if you're lacking in this quality, take stock. Model this behavior if you have to. There is nothing to be afraid of. If you can improve your self-confidence and build yourself up to the point where you truly don't care, then you will be able to put yourself out there and free yourself to be in relationships.

Independence means nothing if you're miserable. Being sexy and confident has nothing to do with isolating yourself and everything to do with getting out there and being the best you can be. It doesn't matter how bright your strong powerful woman vibe is if there's no one else to see it. Remember, life is meant to be lived and when you can find someone who can respect your strength and independence, then sharing it makes it that much enjoyable. So, never make the mistake of confusing independence with isolation. Sexy and confident women don't because they are confident enough to know that people need people and that anyone who looks down on them for this is just missing the point.

IT'S OKAY TO WANT A MAN, BUT…

Everyone gets lonely. Everyone wants someone to share their life with. At least most people do.

But it's another thing entirely to be clingy and desperate. Especially when it comes to a man.

Let's be serious. While every woman wants to be sexy and confident because she wants to be viewed as a very competent and capable person, she also wants to be viewed this way in order to attract good men. And while many people will tell you this is a wrong way to look at things, I'm telling you that it's perfectly okay and completely natural. The only problem is when this need to be viewed as attractive by men turns into desperation or clinginess. This is what usually causes a woman to lower herself in order to "catch" or "keep" a man.

Never put yourself in a position where you need anyone. Especially not a man. Even if you do think you need him, never let him know it. If he catches on, you'll most likely become viewed as one of those women who is desperate—whether you are or not.

So many women make the mistake of throwing themselves at men simply because they think that this is the only way they can attract them. They think that they have to buy them elaborate presents like motorcycles and gold chains. They think that they have to get pregnant in order to get a man to stay. They think that they have become his servant. And what's puzzling to me is that they actually fall for some sort of mental role reversal and start putting the man up on the pedestal. They act as though *they are the suitor!* They act as though they are trying to win the man's heart! This is not how it's supposed to work. Men are supposed to work to get your affections. Not you for theirs. Men are supposed to be the ones who are trying to impress. Women have to go through a lot of bad things in life just by the mere fact of their biology, so why should they have this added burden of having to chase a man too?

But this is all about the desperation that for some reason is so prevalent these days. The odd thing about it is that most of the men for whom these women are supplicating themselves aren't worth it. They are usually incapable, boorish and deadbeats. They are losers. But then again, throughout time, it's always been this type of man that women have chased after. They never seem to chase the good ones. Maybe these types of men just bring out the maternal instinct in women? Who knows? In any case, never put yourself into the position that you absolutely need a man. This is when you look neither sexy nor confident. Instead you look like a complete fool.

You need to keep in mind that no matter how badly you are in love, no matter how lonely you are, and no matter how badly you feel the need for companionship, you can't let a man know that you *need* anything. You can let him know that you want him, but never that you need him. If you let him know this, his ego will go through the roof and you'll spend the rest of your relationship going out of your way to keep his affections. Never upset the balance. The man needs you. You don't need him.

Remember that you are self-sufficient. You can do anything you want. Because of this you don't need anyone to complete you. It's okay to have someone to share your life with and to do nice things for, but when this becomes a case of you feeling that you have to lower yourself just to attract or keep a man, then things have gone south. You're too good for this. A relationship is a two-way street and if you're desperate, you're just putting yourself in a position to be taken advantage of.

Just put yourself out there and be you. If he's attracted, you'll know it. If you're sexy and confident, you won't have to do a thing other than what you're already doing. Remember you don't need anyone. They need you.

A BAD MAN WILL RUIN A GOOD WOMAN

How often have you looked a couple and said to yourself, "She is too good for him." Or you may have wondered, "How did a guy like that get a girl like her?"

There's usually a reason behind this thinking. I hate to say it, but this is what happens when a woman dates below her standards. Sure, there are diamonds in the rough, but many times this type of dating will not bring the substandard man up to her standards but rather her down to his.

I've seen it time and time again. Regardless of how good a woman is, she will be brought down by a bad man. She will end up lower in some way than she was before she started dating the guy. It may be her self-esteem that suffers or it may just be her credit rating. It can happen in many different ways. Whether she dates him or marries him, she is brought down to his level. Through his actions, she is affected. Either she changes her behavior or is simply affected by his behavior she is worse off after she meets him. Remember the old saying about what happens when you lay with dogs? Well, with a bad man, you not only get fleas, but you also might end up in the pound.

A sexy and confident woman does not let this happen. She knows when a man is bad and she either dumps him or avoids him in the first place. She also knows that a relationship is supposed to lift you up, not bring you down. It's about accentuating the best in a couple rather than bringing out the worst.

How a bad man ruins a woman is easy. She falls in love with him. He's not a very good person to begin with, but she either can't or refuses to see it. She thinks either he needs mothering or he's a bad boy living on the edge, or any other various scenarios. She feels she needs to protect him and it usually comes back to haunt her or she thinks he's so cool that she needs to join in on his bad activities. Maybe they get married and then divorced and then out of spite he ruins her credit. Or he ruins her reputation. Or he starts calling her work and saying that she's a drug user. Or he turns the children against her. There are other ways it can happen, but these are the most common.

A good way to avoid this is when you're dating someone, or prospectively dating someone, remember the one question you were asked on all your job interviews and apply it to the person you're dating. Ask yourself where this person will be in five years. Will he be a drug addict? Does he seem vindictive? Does he seem nice? Does he seem like a nice guy? Does he seem cheap? Is he a criminal? Really look at this. I know that you won't be able to know everything about this person, but there will be indicators. If you can do this, you will avoid one of the biggest pitfalls many women make, choosing the wrong man. You don't want to be brought down because you loved the wrong man.

DON'T BE ONE OF THE BOYS

When you're a woman, it's fun to hang out with the guys. It's good to be able to shoot the bull, watch sports on the big screen, drink beer and play pool. No one is arguing this. But you can't forget that you are a woman. And more importantly, you can never let *them* forget that you a woman either. Many girls out there make the mistake of being "one of the boys." While this is good if you want to drink beer, shoot pool and just hang out, it probably won't help your chances of either being perceived as sexy and confident or in attracting the kind of man in whom you're interested. Heterosexual men do not see each other as sexy and confident. If you act too much like one of the boys, you run the risk of not being seen as sexy and confident either.

When you're sexy and confident, there's no danger of this happening because there's no way that they can ever forget that you are one sexy and confident female. You're smart, sure of yourself and not afraid to show your feminine side. You don't have to act like one of the boys because you're perfectly comfortable with the fact that you are a woman. You embrace it. You're being yourself and no man is going to be able to overlook something that great.

However, some women are not so lucky. Some women, especially younger ones, even though they're laid back tomboys at heart, take it for granted that men will know just how feminine they are just by the simple fact of their gender. Many times, men will overlook hot women in their midst if the hot woman is not necessarily presenting herself in this way. It's sad but true and many girls' feelings get hurt because they're getting looked at as one of the guys or as someone's little sister.

It's like this, if you act like one of the boys, you'll be thought of as "one of the boys." This is the end of story and most men, unless they're gay, are not interested in dating one of the boys. If you act like all you're interested in is eating peanuts and drinking beer and playing darts then this is how you'll be treated. If this is okay with you then fine, but if you're more interested in being treated like a lady, then you'll probably be disappointed.

Men like women to be women. They like them to do feminine things. They like women to be interested in girlie things. It's what attracts them. It's what sets you apart from them. If you act like them, why would they be interested in that? Sure, a lot of men might think it's cute that you're interested in all these guy things, but if you don't have a heavy dose of femininity to outweigh it, then you're not going to be putting out the vibe that you're trying to achieve. As with most things, you have to achieve a balance.

And what if you truly are being yourself when you're doing guy things? What if this is the kind of stuff that you like to do? There's nothing wrong with that. However, this needs to be an area of improvement. Even if this is a big part of who you are, there's also a big part that's girlie. You need to emphasize this. You can never let a man forget to treat you like a lady but moreover you can never let a man forget that you *are* a lady.

Of course, there's nothing wrong with hanging out with the fellas every once in a while. Just be sure that you do it as a lady. Don't try to out-guy the guys. Especially if you're interested in a romantic relationship with one of them. The key words are sexy and confident and to be perceived like this, don't let them forget for a second that you're a lady. All too often a girl gets her heart broken by some guy with whom she hangs out. She thinks he's her "one" but he sees her as just a "friend." Why is this? Because they do the stuff that "friends" do. If you hang out with men too much in these kinds of settings, you're going to send mixed messages. The men will get *too* relaxed with you and begin to think that you're one of the fellas.

So keep in mind that if you act like one of the boys too much, you'll be perceived as one of the boys. Not sexy or confident. Men like women to be women. Men like femininity. If you don't put yourself out there as a woman, you're putting yourself at an automatic disadvantage.

THE MALE INFLUENCE IN YOUR LIFE

Did you grow up thinking that a woman's place is at work while a man's is at home sitting on the couch drinking? Or did you grow up thinking that men were emotionally or physically distant? That they stayed to themselves and didn't spend too much time at home except at holidays or birthdays? If then? Did your mother tell you that men were lazy and no good and that you should never get married?

If so, then you've probably have a slightly warped view of men and the role they play in women's lives. This means all men. Including the ones with whom you've had relationships. Without even knowing it, you've probably developed anger and trust issues as a result of these men that you grew up around. If it's all you've known, how are you supposed to know anything else?

While every person is the pilot of their own destiny, so to speak, it may just be possible that the reason why you may be making bad choices in relationships, in particular your choices in men is that this is, once again, simply the way you were brought up. It may be that this is the kind of man you're attracted to simply because this is the kind of men you grew up around. It's what you're used to and because of this, you're cheating yourself out of many more relationships simply because you're ruling out all the good men because they're sort of alien to you. Worthless men are comfortable to you and to step outside of your comfort zone is scary. The end result of all this is that you end up feeling bad about yourself. In other words, not sexy and confident because you're with men that are sucking you dry mentally and emotionally. And this is what you keep going back to again and again.

Think about it. What kind of men did you grow up around? Were they good men? Were they good men, but...*they drank a lot and they didn't work very much?* Or they lay around the house? Or they abused your mother? Or they had "emotional problems?" Or they were troubled? Or they needed mothering? Or they were nice but emotionally unavailable? Or they were workaholics weren't there physically? It goes on and on. Do you see a pattern here? Are these the kinds of men that you're attracting? It's a common saying that women marry men who are like their fathers. While I don't believe this is true all the time, I think there is a lot to this. We go to what we are used to and if this is the kind of man you're used to, then this is the kind of man you'll end up with. That is to say if you don't make an effort to avoid this. The same thing applies to jobs and other aspects of your life. Let's say you always get crappy jobs, the jobs that no one else wants. Why is this? It's because you're the kind of person who is used to these kinds of jobs. If you want a better life, you have to break the pattern and start expecting more for yourself.

Of course no one is perfect and there are no perfect men. Everyone has flaws. However, there are men who have it together. There are men who are hard workers and who are there emotionally and physically. There are men who will make you feel good about yourself. These are the types of men that you need to date. Sure, it may be a little tough at first because you're going to be off balance in the relationship because you've never been treated that well, but just give it time. If you can break the habit of dating bad men, then you'll reap great rewards, not only from a relationship standpoint but also from the fact that your self-esteem and attutude about life will be much better.

So look around you. If you're perennially unhappy in your relationships, it may be because of the men you date. Are they very similar to men that you grew up with? Is this a problem? Just realize that there are good men out there and just because you weren't around that many growing up, this doesn't mean that they don't exist. Stop drifting into the same situations. Just because this is all you know doesn't mean that can't learn anything else. Everyday is a new beginning. You just have to allow yourself to take it.

THE ANGRY GIRL

I don't know if you seen these girls, but if you have you know exactly the ones I'm talking about. They're the ones who are always exploding with rage at everything that doesn't go their way. They're the ones who are always starting fights with other girls and with everyone else in general. They throw tantrums. They run off in a huff. They threaten people in stores. They lose their cool in traffic. They are the ones that people are referring to when they talk about "crazy bitches." They are angry girls. And the problem is that for the most part they don't even know what makes them so angry.

You aren't one of these girls, are you? Do you ever find yourself becoming enraged over unimportant things? Do you act like an overgrown brat? If you are, you need to make some big changes to your outlook if you are going to succeed in life. Because let me tell you, these angry girls are not only annoying, they're also a little scary. They make people nervous just to be around them. I'm sure I'm not alone in this. No one wants to be around someone who is going to explode at every little thing that does not go their way. Sure, in their minds, they may justify their behavior by thinking that they were wronged and mistreated. To them, this may be substantiated by the fact that people sometimes respond to their unusually shrill and loud complaints and give them what they want. But, just bear in mind, this compliance is not because they are right. But merely because they want the angry girl to leave. People don't appreciate people like this. No wants to hire a girl like this and no one wants to date one either.

Yes, no one wants to date one of these girls. Oh, I know that many of these girls are very good looking and have no problem picking up men. The pretty ones are sometimes a little crazy, right? However what these girls don't realize is that one of the reasons why they are so unhappy in their relationships is because most of the men they date get very tired of their "crazy bitch" behavior. The same thing goes with everyone else in their lives as well. They will only be able to get along (or at least think they're getting along) with people who are completely afraid of them. With people who are so cowed down that they will keep their mouths shut and let the rage flow unchecked. After all, who wants to confront one of these girls? They're psycho! Well, not really psycho but their behavior makes people think they are.

What can you do though? What can you do to change? If you can't control your anger? If you're one of these girls? The first thing is to take a step back and try to figure out what exactly it is that is making you angry. Is it jealousy? Is it fear? Is it rejection? Is it fear of rejection? Figure it out. It is probably pretty easy. Whatever it is, it can be overcome. Look back at your life and try to figure out when you became so angry. Was there something that happened to you that caused it? Did you have a major life-changing event? Did something get triggered from your childhood? There is no point in going through life being angry because ultimately people will begin to resent you for it. And they will also avoid you. It doesn't matter how sexy you are, no one wants to always be around a psycho. At least not long-term. Sure, you might get used for your body and looks, but after the beast is unleashed, the door will soon be yours. Guaranteed.

So if you're an angry girl, figure out why. You need to get to the bottom of why you're freaking out when you don't get your way. You need to know why you're acting like such a brat. You also need to realize that no one appreciates it. It doesn't matter how good looking or sexy you are. Being angry all the time is not a sign of confidence. It is a sign of weakness. It is indicative of a person who cannot control herself. Sure, no one in your life may have ever confronted you about this, but you know if this chapter is about you. The thing is that for the most part, the average person is not going to confront you on this. Most people aren't going say anything to you about it. They are just going to leave you alone. Which is not necessarily a good thing. This is why you have to figure this out on your own. Are you an angry girl? If you are, you better get over it soon or you may just have a very unhappy and even angrier rest of your life.

BAD ROLE MODELS

What you know, you become. Usually.

We have already talked about how history can repeat itself in that one of the reasons why you may be having so many bad relationships is because this is all you know. Also, as I have mentioned before, a reason why you may not be the woman you want to be is because of bad examples. In other words, people who you were around when you were growing up may still be having an effect on how you are now. While men are sometimes the culprits in this because many women seek the same old substandard ones over and over again because of the men earlier in your childhood, many times it's your female role models who are to blame. If you grew up with desperate and subservient women, then chances are you will act like this to a certain extent.

It's true. If you're having problems with men it may be because your mother had the same problems. What you know, you become. No one can fault you for this either. You probably didn't even know it was happening.

Everyone loves their mothers (or at least I hope they do), but sometimes mom may not have made the best choices in men. She may not have really stood up for herself as much as she should have. Did she take a lot of crap? Was she a happy person? What about grandma? Was she always complaining about the men in her life? It may be painful for you to think about this, especially if it entails you also looking at the male role models in your life, but you need to do this. If you take a good look around, you'll probably see where a lot of your behavior comes from. Now, I'm not saying that you should blame everyone for your problems, but you should at least know why you do some of the things and make some of the bad decisions you do. Once you do that, you should become self-aware enough to start making a difference in your own life.

The point is that if you just see where your behavior comes from, then you can realistically question it. You can look at your attitudes that you have previously taken for granted and see that maybe they're not the best ones to have in regards to men or relationships. If you can fix the behavior that is holding you back, you can really start to move forward with your life. You can start to gain the confidence you're lacking. You can also apply this same to knowledge to everything else in your life. You can see why you're afraid to stand up for yourself in the workplace. You can see where any number of behaviors that hold you back come from. I know doing this has certainly helped in my life.

So look around at your female role models. If you grew up witnessing unhappy women with problems then chances are you'll be in a similar situation. You may just be repeating the same behavior without even knowing why you're doing it. Many people go through their whole lives without ever asking themselves why they do certain things. But they should. Anything that holds you back from achieving the most you can should be questioned. Usually it's something that is completely unnecessary or can be fixed easily. Being sexy and confident is a frame of mind and can be achieved without that much effort if you can just remove the behaviors that are blocking you. Take stock and figure out if your female role models are what are holding you back. You can't make changes until you know what's wrong or where the problems are coming from. After that, the world is yours.

GOOD AND DECENT MEN

If you've ever wondered why most of your relationships turn out horribly, you might want to take a look at the men with whom you're having them. If you date horrible men, you're going to have a horrible relationship. End of story. But would things be different if you dated a good man? Would you be happier in your relationship? Most likely, the answer is yes.

But then again, this is fairly obvious, right? At least I hope it is. Because if it's not, then you need to seriously reevaluate how you date.

If bad relationships are continually happening to you, maybe the underlying problem may not necessarily be the men, but rather your taste in men. Maybe you're just drawn to substandard men. Maybe you just have a soft spot for the bad boy or the unemployed. Or the drug user. Or the alcoholic. Or it could be that you're just too focused on the hot sex that you overlook the fact that the guy is a mean bastard. But most likely, you just never look beyond what you already know and just keep dating the same men because these kinds are so familiar. You just overlook the fact that they are so familiarly disappointing and as a result think all men are bad. This causes you to just go through life thinking that all relationships are supposed to be this hard.

We discussed how important is that you keep your bad history from repeating already. We've discussed your female role models and we've discussed why you may be attracted to these less than desirable men, at least less than desirable from a relationship standpoint. What we need to talk about here is what you can do to change it. What can you do to meet a different type of men?

The main question you need to ask yourself is where do you usually meet the men that you're date? Is it in bars? Is it through friends? Friends with questionable tastes themselves, perhaps? This might be your first indicator of what's wrong in your dating life. If you're meeting men in places where questionable men hang out, chances are you're going to meet more questionable men than you would have otherwise. To remedy this, you need to start looking elsewhere. If you're religious, maybe look into church singles groups. If you're not religious, maybe start look into some civic organizations. Look into volunteering at some charitable groups. After all, a man who's volunteering probably isn't all bad, is he? I don't necessarily advise looking for a man in the workplace, but if good things happen there, then so be it. Just exercise some caution. If the guy you date turns out to be a psycho, remember you're going to be working with a psycho.

The thing is to look in a place where good decent men are. Don't look at where the deadbeats are in full effect. If you can avoid these awful, deficient men, then you're well on your way to meeting a good one. I know this may be easier said than done because most likely, you've probably developed some serious trust issues due to your dealings with deadbeats. However, you have to get out there. If you're having trouble trusting and putting yourself out there, just forget that you are dealing with good men. Pretend that they're the deadbeats. You certainly don't have a problem with that do you? Of course, that I'm being facetious here, but I hope that you can see how ridiculous this situation can be. A woman will readily date a loser, but shy away from a good man because of trust. If the issue is that you don't think you deserve better, then you need to realize that you do. You deserve much better. You deserve to have a happy relationship. Don't ever think otherwise. A sexy and confident woman deserves to date a good and decent man. If all she can get is losers, then she is better off alone.

The next thing you need to do is to establish some rules and guidelines in the men that you seek. You need to figure out what exactly is a good and decent man to you. You need to know what qualities in a man will define this for you. Do you want a man who is good with children? Do you want a man who is chivalrous? Do you want a man who is kind to his mother? Just figure out what defines a good man to you. After that, you need to use this information to develop disqualifying factors in men that will either mark them off before you go out with them or will cause you not to go out with them again. Maybe the fact that he cheated on his last girlfriend is a big negative. Maybe he's mean to his dog. Maybe he's too self-centered. Regardless, figure out what's important to you in a man and if you perceive something that's diametrically opposed to this belief, use it to disqualify him.

As I already said, a sexy and confident woman deserves a good and decent man in her life. She deserves the best. She deserves to be happy in a relationship and a big part of this is finding someone that will complement you rather than bring you down. If you can just do these simple things that I have mentioned, you'll find that the quality of men you're meeting will rise dramatically. Look beyond what you're familiar with because what you're familiar with is awful. It may be a little tough at first, but when you start dating good men, your confidence will improve and you'll feel so much better about yourself. You just have to get out of your rut.

This rut is probably one that you've been in all your life, but if you can just raise your head and peek out of it and see what else the world has to offer, you'll be much better off. You'll also stop dating so many losers.

MAKE MEN TREAT YOU LIKE A LADY

Have you ever noticed that men simply aren't very chivalrous anymore?

It's true. They don't hold the door. They don't doff their hats when a woman enters a room. They don't really do much of anything to recognize that a woman is in their presence. In fact, with the way they act nowadays, it's almost like, to them, there's no difference between women and men. It's as though now that everybody is equal, they should be treated the same in every way. The sad thing about it is that women let them get away with it. And what's even sadder is that many women even encourage this kind of thing because they think that it's a sign of equality. They think that if men treat them like just like they treat other men, then they are truly being seen as equals. What is even worse is that this kind of behavior doesn't just stay in the workplace, but also carries over to the dating world as well.

But a sexy and confident woman doesn't think like this. She doesn't want to be treated like a man.

One of the biggest differences between a sexy and confident woman and other women is the fact that men treat a sexy and confident woman like a lady—and she lets them. Moreover she expects them to do this. And they want to do it because they want to be in her good graces. They want her to like them.

Yes, you heard me. She lets them do it. She does this because she knows that it's not a bad thing to be treated well and with respect. It doesn't mean that she is beneath him. In fact, it probably means that he is putting her on a bit of a pedestal. It doesn't make her any less effective at work or anywhere else. It just means that she expects to be treated well and is treated well. She, as well as everybody else, knows men and women are different. She knows that there is a natural order of things with humans and doesn't try to override it with any sort of misplaced sense of politically correctness. Sure, men and women are equal. No one's arguing that. However, there are differences and these shouldn't be overlooked. Also, these differences, in no way, make a woman less than a man.

The problem a lot of women have with being treated like a lady is the fact that so much of the "women's lib" and "independent woman" stuff has been drummed into them that they feel inferior if men recognize them as being women. I hate to say this, but this is the truth. Sure, women should be treated as equals but they should not be treated like men. This is the mistake that many women make. They think that if they act like ladies, then men will look down on them as being weak or prissy. I say embrace being a woman. Let men recognize it and put you on a pedestal. Women have to put up with a lot of bad stuff so take all the good stuff you can out of life. Women have to go through the great pain of childbirth. They have all sorts of issues that men never have to even think about. This is why men have put women on a pedestal throughout history. These burdens haven't been taken away from women either. They're still there. The only difference is that the pedestal is gone and the women are the ones who have removed it.

One thing that a lot of these women who want to be treated like men don't realize is that many small-minded and mean men are using this sense of empowerment and equality against them. They use it as a way of not paying for a woman's dinner on a date. They use it as a way to get around being a gentleman. It's almost as though they're using the fact that women are sometimes treated well and placed on a pedestal against them and they're going to do everything they can to knock them off it. Don't let this happen to you. If a man doesn't treat you like a lady, he isn't worth the trouble to talk to, much less date.

Now for the hard part, how exactly do you get a man to treat you like a lady? The answer is that you expect to be treated like a lady. You also *allow* them to treat you like a lady. You don't have to be mean about it, but if a man acts ungentlemanly, you subtley let him know about it. You can raise an eyebrow or simply excuse yourself from his presence. You have to realize that most men have been taught by society to be somewhat gentlemanly towards women. The problem is that since they are not expected to do so, they don't. This is why you have to expect this treatment. Give them the opportunity to get the door and they will most likely get it the next time. Wait for them to open your door so they get the hint. It will eventually sink in to them that you're not one of the boys and shouldn't be treated as such. In today's socieity, it may take some effort on your part, but you can get the treatment you deserve.

Let men treat you like a woman, not a man wearing a skirt. As I have said earlier, men don't look at each other as being sexy and confident so acting like one isn't going to help your purpose. Never forget that you are equal to a man when it comes to pay and ability, however, don't let this cloud the fact that you are a lady and deserve to be treated as such.

THE SAME MISTAKES OVER AND OVER AGAIN

I know I keep saying this, but don't be a prisoner of your past. Whether it's your childhood, bad role models, or whatever, don't let your past dictate your present and your future.

But some people had great childhoods and had great role models, you may say. What is it that makes these people so miserable in their relationships? Why can't they find good men? Why can't they be happy? I say that this is just another example of the same thing. Except in this case, it's not a case of history repeating, it's a case of your behavior that is being repeated. In other words, you are making the same mistakes over and over again.

Too many people in this world are the victims of their same mistakes that keep repeating over and over again. They wonder why things are always going wrong for them, but yet they keep doing the same things that cause the bad things to happen. If this is you, you have to break this pattern. Yes, it's a pattern and like most of the bad stuff in your life, this kind of behavior, many times, is merely a habit. It's just the way that you do things. Maybe you got started off on the wrong foot back in high school and found that you were only attracted to jerks. Maybe you just don't know any other way to date except to let yourself be used for your body. Regardless, you can change. You can gain your confidence. You can feel sexy without being slutty. You can do it. Everyone is capable of positive changes in their lives. You're no exception

As with most methods of self-improvement, you start this process by self-examination. First you have to figure out what it is that keeps going wrong for you and then trace it back to where it started. Do this with other similar situations. Eventually, you'll see a pattern. As I keep saying, all you have to do is start questioning the areas of your life that make you unhappy and the behavior that is causing it. Whether it's yours or the person with whom you're in a relationship. Then you can start doing things differently. You can see that maybe the reason why you always end up with bad men is because that's the kind to whom you're attracted. Maybe you can see why your men always drain you dry financially is because you start off by giving them money and support and excuse their own lack of ambition. Maybe you can try to begin qualifying the men you date a little better. Make sure that they have ambition. That they have jobs. That they're financially self-secure. That they haven't been in prison. Most problems are easily solved if you're willing to take a long hard look at yourself and then have the discipline to follow through with changing your behavior. Remember the world is yours. You just have to have the guts to be able to take it. Most of the time, this can start with you being able to take control of your life.

If you're going to be sexy and confident, you have to know your weaknesses. It is only through this self-knowledge that you can improve yourself. It is only by knowing the mistakes that you're making that you can make the positive changes in your life which will enable you to stop making them.

SEXY DOES NOT MEAN SLUTTY

I know that women like to dress up and be sexy. I know they like to show off their assets and have fun being feminine. I think this is great, but sometimes you have to know when to say when. You have to know that there's a line that you can cross when you're trying to be sexy. If you cross it, you end up in a whole different territory.

At the risk of sounding old-fashioned, you see many women nowadays, especially young women, who are dressing way too inappropriately and provocatively. Even when they're just going to the grocery store or to the bank, their cleavage is prominently showing and their skirts are way too high. In other words, they are dressing like sluts. Does this mean that there are simply more prostitutes out there than there used to be? Does it mean that there are more girls working the streets? No, it does not. It just means that many women today can no longer differentiate between sexy and slutty. They think that they are dressing sexily (which they are, just not exactly in the best way they can) and that it's okay. They just think it's the fashion these days because somewhere along the line, club-wear has been confused with day-wear. You can't blame these girls. Many of them truly think that they are just following the trends. They don't know that they're giving off the wrong impression. They're on display and most of these girls don't even know they're doing anything wrong.

Now, I'm not a prude. I don't think girls should cover up completely. But you have to use some restraint. Sexy and slutty are very different but it is a fine line between them. While fashions come and go and clothes get more daring, there are some tried and true rules to know when you're going too far.

- Sexy hints and slutty shows. In other words, sexy shows just a bit, while slutty is on full display.
- Sexy can fit in anywhere. Slutty only can go to the clubs.

There are other ways of telling if you're overdone, but these two tips should help you. The number one thing is could you wear this outfit somewhere other than a club? If you can, chances are you're sexy instead of slutty.

When I say these things, I'm not making any moral judgments. This has nothing to do with whether you're a good or bad person. What I'm talking about is that you need to know how to dress if you want to give off a good impression and stay safe. I know that it shouldn't really matter how you dress and that you should be able to show whatever you want. However, not everyone thinks this way. Men and jealous other women will judge you. Men may even try to hurt you over what you're wearing because they get the wrong idea about you. They think that since you're on display, then you're ripe for the taking. Of course, this is due to the faulty thinking of these people, but why take the risk? It's not worth it. Don't be the girl who gives a creep the wrong impression just because she's just having fun showing off her assets.

But what about when you're going out to the clubs? Sure, you might want to dress a little more sexily, but just try to show some restraint. Not just because you don't want to give off the wrong impression, but because of the weird, creepy men I mentioned earlier. You don't want them to get any wrong ideas about you. You don't want them thinking just because you're going panty-less, this means that you're ready for action—with whoever comes along. Just use your best judgment and try not to go too far with your outfit.

Just keep in mind that sexy is a hint of cleavage and/or a little leg. Maybe your shoulders. Slutty just bares all and shamelessly lets it all hang out—literally. If you can differentiate between the two, you'll grow into your sexiness and will become a much more confident woman.

HOW TO DRESS SEXILY AND CONFIDENTLY

As I've mentioned several times already, how you present yourself is crucial. It's how people form their first impressions and many times it's very hard to ever change these once they are formed. This is why you can never appear desperate. However, there's more to it than this. If you're going to be viewed as sexy and confident, you have to make *that* first impression too. And what you wear will play a big part in this.

How a girl dresses is a big part of how she is perceived. Her clothes will largely determine just how people think of her. Whether she's looked at as a frump or a tart, it all has to do with her first impression. While appearances shouldn't matter, in the real world they do. Think about it, what do you look at first when you see someone? Their hair? Their shoes? Of course, you look at these things. How a person dresses is important and it's very hard to see past a person's fashion blunders.

While we've talked about the difference between sexy and slutty, we haven't discussed the clothing aspect of this in regards to showing that you are feminine and secure. Just, how do you dress both sexily and confidently? So that you can show that you are indeed sexy but are still to be taken seriously? It's a fine line that you're walking but it is possible. As is the key to being both sexy and confident, you have to strike a balance. You have to go far enough, without going too far. You have to put yourself out there without going *too far* out there.

I'm not going to tell you specific items to wear because styles come and go, but the biggest thing is for you to be comfortable with what you're wearing. If you're self-conscious about your clothes, it will show and you will not appear as confident as you should. That being said, this doesn't mean that you should cover up and hide. You do need to push yourself a little if you're the jeans and sweatshirt type. To be sexy, you don't have to show everything. You just need to hint at your sexuality. A little bit of cleavage goes a long way as does just a little bit of leg. You don't want to overdo it because then people will not take you seriously. However, if you completely cover up all the time, you'll look like a prude. You have to dress like a woman who is not ashamed of the fact that she is a woman. Don't be afraid to tastefully show off your curves. You also can't be too overly concerned with making comfort your goal. Sure, you shouldn't be uncomfortable, but if you are too much of a slouch, people will probably get the impression that you're either lazy or ashamed of your body.

As a woman, men (and other women) will expect you to dress like a woman. And age appropriately. You will not get points for dressing younger or older than what you are. You are expected to look your best and be not only age appropriate but also situation appropriate. In other words, don't wear a bikini to church. Just joking, but you get my point.

As I mentioned in another chapter, the thing you need to do is play to your strengths. Accentuate the best parts of yourself when it comes to how you dress. If you have nice legs, show them off a little. If you have a nice body, wear something a little more form-fitting. Just don't overdo it. If you're the type who likes to really show it off, try to restrain yourself a little. You'll accomplish more with showing less. Just don't go too far and venture into muumuu land.

So the thing is to achieve a balance. Dress so that you are confident in what you are wearing and know that you can pull it off, but don't cover up and hide. Play to your strengths so that you can be sexy without feeling like you're on display. Dress like a woman who is proud of the fact that she is a woman. Remember just a hint of sexiness and you'll be okay.

YOU HAVE TO BE REALISTIC

Like most women, you probably grew up dreaming of Prince Charming. Your idea of the perfect man was forged in the fairy tales of your childhood. He would be a man who was everything a girl could possibly dream about. He would be handsome, charming, chivalrous and rich. And to make things even better, he would also be able to save the day. He would be your dreamboat. However, as you grew older, you probably outgrew Prince Charming. However, you didn't outgrow the concept. Over time, through the influence of romance novels and romantic comedies, he slowly transformed into "The One" or "Mr. Right." Regardless of what you called him, though, he was just another version of Prince Charming, except without the fairy tale setting. As a result of all this sort of programming that all little girls and young women go through, you've probably always been disappointed by almost every man you've ever dated. This has probably also carried over to other aspects of your life. Nothing ever seems to measure up to the way it does in the movies, does it? In other words, your reality is not matching up to the reality you think you're seeing for everyone else. Or at least the one you've been shown to be real on the television. It makes you feel *less than*. How are you going to feel sexy and confident if you think that you don't have it as good as everybody else does?

The problem is that you're not being realistic. You're trying to live up to a standard that isn't real. Instead of trying to be the best you that you can be, you're trying to be something that is impossible for anyone to be because it doesn't actually exist. You're looking at a world that seems to have none of the problems that you have. That is much more glamorous and exciting than the one that you have. That is filled with perfect men and is so much easier and less complicated. What you're overlooking is that this world doesn't exist. It is not real. Everyone in real life has problems with something and if you beat yourself up for being normal, then you're just going to feel badly about yourself.

It's true. Do you ever find yourself thinking that things in your life just aren't that great? Do you think that that you would be so much happier if only such and such had happened? Or you had this or that? Or if you had only met "The One." Don't feel like the Lone Ranger about this. Everyone feels this way. However, the thing you need to ask yourself is this: Are you looking at your life realistically? Are the things that you think would make you happy actually things that could naturally occur in your life? In other words are you being realistic in what you're expecting out of life?

For example, do you think you could be happy only if you live in a mansion? Do you over look the home you have and take it for granted simply because it's not like one you've seen on television? Do you think your job is crap because it's crap or simply because it's not glamorous or makes you ridiculously rich? These are all questions that you need to ask yourself. Everyone can do better, this is for sure, but to take what you have for granted just because it's not like something you've seen on television or the movies will just make you miserable. You have to realize that such thinking is rooted in low self-esteem. It's just like all the other things in your life that will sabotage you and your confidence. If you're confident in yourself, you will want more out of life, however, you will not put yourself down because you have yet to achieve your goals. You will take nothing for granted because you will have worked for everything you have gotten. If you have it, you deserved it. It is not crap.

A sexy and confident woman is realistic about her life. She's appreciates what she has because she's earned it. She does not put herself down because she is not living in a fairy tale. If anyone else looks down on her because she has not yet achieved a high level of success, then that is merely an indicator of their own shallowness and low self-esteem.

AUTOPILOT

Have you ever noticed that most people go through life according to a routine? They get up, go to work and come home. Then on the weekend, if they're not working, they go out or sleep in. Or some variant of this. This is not necessarily a bad way to be, however, if you are not careful, you will become a prisoner of this routine. You will get so that you're either too afraid to break it or get so indoctrinated into it that you just don't want to. It's comfortable. It's easy and you can do it without even thinking. In other words, you're on autopilot and that's just fine by you.

At least for now it is. Do you really think that you'll feel the same way in twenty years? Do you really think that you won't look back and wish that maybe you should have taken a few chances? Do you think that you're going to look back at the rut that your life has become and wish that maybe you might have at least thought about trying to get out of it?

If you are to do something better with your life in regards to dating and jobs, you're going to have to start doing things differently. Obviously, right? But saying you're going to do something differently and actually doing something differently are two completely different things. It takes effort and it takes a little bravery. It also takes the ability to be able to not be discouraged if everything doesn't work out perfectly.

The problem many people have with improving themselves is the fact that they usually have to leave their comfort zone to do it. This can sometimes be a very scary thing for most. If you want evidence of this, just look at people who make New Year's resolutions. Sure, they start out with the best of intentions, but when push comes to shove they usually just go back to the same behavior. Of course, there are those who do succeed, but as human beings, we usually tend towards the comfortable and the known.

Being in a rut can mean many things to many people. To some people it may mean that they're dating the same type of man over and over again. To others it may mean that they keep making the same mistakes in relationships or they're just sick of their job routine.Nevertheless, if you're tired of your routine, you need to change it. And you need to do it as soon as possible.

When it comes to ruts in regards to the way women feel about themselves, a couple of problems that happen to women who are trying to improve themselves by becoming sexy and confident. Some are too afraid to put themselves out there for fear of rejection. They think if they leave the safe confines of the shadows and their frumpy, mousy clothes that they will get too much attention. They're afraid that people will actually start to notice them! And on the other hand you have the ones who like to show it off too much. They think that if they reign in their sexuality just a bit so that people take them more seriously then men will stop looking at them altogether. These situations are just two sides of the same coin. They both have to do with the attention women receive. Both types of girls need to realize that there is a middle ground. There is a place where a woman can land where men won't start drooling over them and also not be so repulsed that they run away to join a monastery. This is why you have to get out of the rut you're in. Typically, it's one variation of this outlook or the other that is holding women back.

Let's face it, even if the above scenarios don't apply to you, you're probably fairly tired of the routine that you have. You've probably been in it for years and go through it every week. Meanwhile you keep getting more and more bored and unhappy with it. If this is the case, what better reason do you have for getting out of your rut? At least you won't be as bored with your life.

Just bear this in mind when you start making positive changes in your life, you will be plunging into the unknown. You will be doing different things. You may even fail at some of them. This is not bad. This is good. The important thing is that you should keep trying different things until you are pleased with your life. If you're so happy with the way things are, you wouldn't be reading this book, would you? So keep in mind that good change is good. A bad habit will fight you when you try to break it so that's why you must know that you're doing good and keep doing it until it becomes the new routine or a new better habit.

JEALOUSY

People are always their own worst enemies. We're always doing things that ultimately sabotage ourselves. We just can't help it. It's like it doesn't matter how well things are going, we just can't stop ourselves from doing that one thing that brings it all down. And usually we aren't even aware we're doing it. Jealousy is just one example of this. Sure, we have to worry about car crashes, wild dog attacks and subway muggings too, but if those don't get us, then ultimately we will do something to not necessarily harm us physically, but will work to undermine how we feel about ourselves and the world around us. This is where jealousy comes in.

Yes, jealousy. It is one of the biggest things that sabotage people and I think women are more susceptible to it than men. The reason for this probably lies in the fact that many women suffer from low self-esteem. They see imagined slights and rivalries everywhere. They are threatened by anything and anyone that they see as being better than they are. Rightly or wrongly. Since they also usually suffer from low self-esteem, the focus of this jealousy can come from a lot of areas. They become jealous of other women. They resent their boyfriend/husband's friends. They are jealous of people on television who they think have better stuff or better situations than them. The list is endless. As a result, this jealousy makes some women look low, bitter and mean.

It can also make them act crazy and do things that they may not do normally. It also means that they are making what they are most afraid of a reality. By being envious of others and allowing it to make them behave badly, they are in effect becoming lower than the people of whom they are jealous. Or least they appear so. It makes people around them wonder if maybe there's a reason behind this resentment.

Why women have low self-esteem is anyone's guess. I'm not a psychologist but I do have some opinions which I get into in a later chapter of the book. I think it's most likely rooted in childhood and the fact that they're always told that they're not as capable as the boys are. Regardless of cause though, you have to realize that jealousy and self-esteem are behind so many of the ills in this world that have been committed. Look at home invasions. Look at random attacks on people. Look at careers which have been destroyed by rivalries. Why do you think that many of these things come about? I'll tell you, they come about because at one point in the timeline of these events one person felt that someone else had something they didn't and they didn't like it. Instead of striving to get this thing for himself the right way, he decided to take it away from the person who had it. Or completely destroy it. This way no one has anything that could make him feel inferior.

If you don't think I'm right just look around any office situation. Look at the way the older women treat the younger ones. Especially the prettier girls. Notice the snarky comments. Notice how the older women will sabotage the younger ones. Notice how they'll go to any length to make them look bad or get them fired. This is because of pure jealousy. It would seem as a woman gets older that she would gain more of a sense of herself and her purpose, but in reality the opposite usually occurs. Her self-esteem gets even lower and she gets even bitterer. Don't be like this. If you're the jealous type then it will not get any better unless you make the effort to stop it.

But what about jealousy in regards to boyfriends and husbands? What about jealousy in regards to how women react towards them? This one is a little different but is still rooted in insecurity. This one will be harder to overcome but if you can accept that a little territoriality is natural, you'll be okay. You just can't let it go too far and let it destroy you or your opinion of yourself. You can let it make you feel insecure. Also you have to realize that it really has nothing to do with you. Your man's behavior is his own. Not yours. If he wants to look at another woman, then let him. You're the commodity. If he wants to flirt with another woman, he needs to realize that it is hurtful to you and makes you look bad. You have to communicate this. However, you should also keep in mind that you're a beautiful woman who can get any man she wants. So if he wants to play this game then he can move on. Another one will be in later. You see, it's all about self-esteem. If you have the confidence to know that you don't need him if he misbehaves, then you'll understand. You can't control other people's behavior, only your own. This is what you have to realize. You can't let it make you crazy.

It goes without saying but I'm going to say it anyway jealousy is the opposite of confidence. It also is not very sexy. It makes a woman look weak and bitchy. It will make you appear to become what made you jealous to begin with—inferior. It is a self-perpetuating quality that will only grow if you feed it. You have to stop it before it gets started. It will also lead to a lot of alone time if she doesn't watch out because no one wants to be around someone who is like this. Also, no man wants to date a crazy jealous woman. At least not for long.

Here's a tip on how to cope with jealousy when it comes to material things: When you see that someone has something that you want, don't feel inferior or wish the worst on them. Let it inspire you to get it on your own. Remember a rising tide raises all boats. When something good happens to someone around you, it means that it's possible that it can happen to you too. And when you're jealous of another woman over a man? You need to realize that you're the commodity. If he doesn't think that your feelings are worth anything, then he's not worth anything. Don't ever chase a man. Let him go. Don't let it make you crazy. Once he sees that you don't care what he does, then you'll only be looked at as that much stronger of a person.

So the next time, you feel that twinge of jealousy, think about it. Is it really warranted? Are you really that threatened? I think if you really mull it over, you'll find that you really don't have anything to envy or be afraid of at all. Embrace others. This includes their strengths, economic gains and good fortune. Just because someone else is doing well doesn't mean that you can't and it also doesn't mean that you have to feel like you're less than them. If you can stop being jealous, you'll not only begin to look much better to other people, but you'll also start feeling much better about yourself as well. This is the key to being sexy and confident.

DATING CONFIDENTLY

When you're a confident person, you will apply this confidence to all aspects of your life. You will be able to use it in the workplace, at home and in your relationships. It will improve everything about you because you will not longer be overwhelmed by doubt. When you're confident, you know where you're going and if you don't, you know who to ask.

So what does this have to do with dating? Well, everything. Because if you can learn to date confidently, you'll not only date better, but you will most likely be able to achieve success.

It's like this, many people date. However, few date confidently. There's a reason for this. It's because those who date confidently usually find partners more quickly because they know what they're looking for and they know when they've found it. They're not out there questioning themselves and going through the whole "I love you, but I'm not in love with you" thing. They don't waste their time because they know what they're looking for. They're not so insecure that they depend on the affections of people who don't really love them.

This is what dating confidently means. It means that you know what you're looking for. You know the qualities and the type of individual that you're in search of. More importantly, you're not afraid to seek this person out. It also means that you can prioritize. If a person has all the qualities that you're looking for but is lacking in a few, you don't just throw him away. You look at the whole picture because you're confident enough to know that you're going to make a good decision. You're not wishy-washy or looking for "The One." You're looking for a good person who fulfills the criteria you're looking for. You're looking for a person you're attracted to and you're not going to let the fact that he's not perfect get in the way. You're not going to waste your time on a fixer-upper, but if the guy in whom you're interested is only in need of a wardrobe update, then you can handle that without any problem. You know what works for you and what you can handle. And what you won't put up with. Of course, dating confidently also means that you can cut someone loose who isn't quite up to snuff.

To date confidently you must evaluate your standards. Are they too high? Are they too low? Are you looking for "Mr. Right?" Or are you looking the "The One?" If you fall into any of these categories, then you're going to be spending a lot of time alone. Or, at least dating a lot of guys who you will subsequently find lacking. Do you even have standards? Or do you just go with whoever asks you just because you don't want to hurt anybody's feelings? If you're going to date confidently, you have to look at what's important and why it's important. Do you expect a man to be kind? Or are looks your thing? If looks are what you're mainly after, expect to be ultimately disappointed because looks are only skin deep, as they say. And if your good-looking guy doesn't have more substantitive qualities like a kind heart or loyalty then you will have a lot of hurt in your relationship. In other words, you have to check more than one box when you're looking at men.

Know what you want and be willing to prioritize. These are the keys to successful dating. Follow your heart and your head. If you like a guy but he doesn't fulfill every quality you're looking for then see what happens. Maybe he's not so bad after all. However, if you know for a fact that he's no good and are just following your hormones, expect to be home alone crying some time soon. Date as if you know what you want. Because you do know what you want out of a man. You just have to admit it to yourself. You know what's important to you. Stop waffling and start dating confidently!

PLAY TO YOUR STRENGTHS

Do you ever see successful and confident people doing really badly at things? Of course, you might see basketball players and actors sucking at celebrity golf and tennis tournaments, but that's for charity and is expected. What I'm talking about is real life. Using the same line of thinking, do you ever see sexy, confident and successful people really looking bad?

Of course not. This is because they always play to their strengths. They accentuate the good things about themselves in public and work on the weaker ones in private. This is one of the main reasons why we have the perception that they're sexy and confident in the first place.

Everybody has stuff they're good at. Everybody has good features. Everybody has areas in which that they excel. You're no exception. You do have great things about yourself that make you stand apart from the crowd. You have wonderful features that are appealing to men and you have skills that are welcome in any workplace. Whether or not, you're doing anything with them is not within my ability to tell. However, if you're not using these to their utmost potential, you should start. Without doing harm to anyone else, you need to always put yourself in the best light possible. This is why when you do anything in life, always play to your strengths. While this is true of your skills, it's also very true of your looks and physical attributes.

It's like this. Instead of hiding or covering up what you perceive to be the bad things about yourself, accentuate the good things that set you apart from the crowd. When you do this it will make people only notice the good parts and ignore the weaker ones. Do you have stuff you're good at when it comes to dating or interacting with others? Are you a good cook? Do you have pretty eyes? Are you friendly? Do you make people feel comfortable? Do you have nice legs? I think you know where I'm going. This is the stuff you need to emphasize. Too many people waste so much of their time trying to cover their flaws that all the good stuff about them gets overlooked. It's like people who wear large sweatshirts trying to cover their stomachs. Sure, you don't see the stomach, but all you notice about them is the sweatshirt. You don't even notice their hair or eyes.

Of course, I'm not saying that you shouldn't work on your flaws. Everyone can make improvements. However, you should always remember your strong points and let them be the feature you lead with. Whether it's an ability you have or a facet of your personality, you will always feel more comfortable doing something you're good at. You will feel more confident. This confidence will always carry you through. If you can just remember this, you will do well in life. The added benefit to this is that if you stop worrying so much about things that you're trying to hide or are uncomfortable with, you'll find that with the pressure off, these things may just start becoming less important and less noticeable. Especially to you.

Of course, as I mentioned earlier, when you begin putting yourself in a good light, you should never do it in a way that puts other people down. Never lord over or put down the less enlightened. Many women will never know this secret to looking sexy and confident and if you make yourself look good at their expense, you'll only diminish yourself in many people's eyes. Look your best but do it on your own terms. Never do it at anyone's expense.

Remember to always play to your strengths. They're your strengths for a reason. You'll not only feel sexier and confident when you're doing this, you'll also find that your weaknesses may just not be so weak after all.

SEXY DOESN'T COME IN A GLASS

Everybody likes to kick loose and have a good time. It's when you start having to drink to have this good time that you're heading into dangerous territory. No matter how sexy or confident you may feel after a few cocktails, chances are that people around you aren't getting that same impression of you.

Yes, I know that it's sometimes hard to get out there and talk to new people. I know that it's hard to sometimes try new things. I also know that this is why so many women—and men, too for that matter—drink too much when they are in social situations. It's called liquid courage for good reason, but when you rely too much upon it, you just end up looking like a drunk and maybe getting so "courageous" that you end up doing something that later you wish you hadn't. I also know that drinking too much makes you neither sexy or confident despite how you might feel while under the influence.

It's true. Drinking can be a crutch in social situations. I have nothing against having a drink or two while at a party, but when it gets to be the only way that you can get out there and talk to people, then you might want to think about taking it down a notch. You might want to think about maybe not drinking so much in the future.

Men get drunk all the time in public, right? But how are they perceived? As drunks or as loudmouthed idiots, usually. To be a sexy confident woman, you should not be perceived as either. You have to put out the impression that you are in full control. A glass of wine doesn't make you into a fool. This is why you need to know your limits. If you don't, then you will most probably do a lot of stuff you regret. You'll give men the time of day who usually wouldn't rate a second glance. You will go home with men who do not live up to your standards and much worse. You won't exercise the caution that you usually would in such circumstances and you may end up making mistakes that you'll regret for a lifetime. Sure, you might have a good time during, but what about afterwards? If you had only exercised a little moderation, then you would feel much better about yourself in the morning.

I know how it usually starts for most people. When they're either in high school or college, they discover this great thing called alcohol. It's wonderful at first because it helps eliminate shyness and makes you bolder. It allows the bashful person to go up to complete strangers and introduce themselves and more. It makes the things that normally intimidate you not so scary and eventually becomes a great way to have a good time when you're out. However, over time, using alcohol as a social lubricant will just become too easy. It will also become a little boring and predictable. It's just a crutch. If you can develop the skills to be as bold and conversational without alcohol, just think how great it would be. You truly would be courageous then and you would be doing it on your own.

Sure, it easier to have a few drinks to get loosened up, but you have to know your limits. You also know that as a woman, your tolerance for alcohol will be considerably less than that of the men you will be around. If you can just make it a habit of introducing yourself and having a good time without being intoxicated, you'll find that soon enough you won't need that bracer to get you started. This way, you will actually start really enjoying parties and other social functions as well.

REGARDLESS OF WHAT YOU THINK, YOU'RE ATTRACTIVE

I know you do this. Everyone does. Whenever you look in the mirror you can't help but see all your flaws. You overlook all the good stuff and go directly to the stuff about you that might be less than perfect. The same thing goes for the rest of your life as well. You only focus on the not-so-perfect stuff and ignore everything else that's good. The problem with this is that you may be the only person out there who agrees with you. Yes, that's right. What you think is unattractive is most likely not unattractive at all.

Attraction is relative. What we may consider unattractive about ourselves, someone else *will* find attractive. Some women are obsessed that their noses are too big. However, there are many men out there who either don't care about such things or will find these noses very attractive. Men live in the real world, too. They understand that people have flaws and the ones who are looking for "perfect" women will probably end up alone. They also love the little quirks that make women unique. They love the things that make them different from everybody else. I've seen some women even complain that their hair is too curly. I've got news for you. Men love curly hair. And on the other hand, I've heard some women complain about having hair that's too straight. I've got more news for you. Men love straight hair too. Men who love women love women regardless.

And what does this mean to you? It means that regardless of your flaws, you're attractive. Let this sink in. If you think you're fat, skinny or in-between, there is a man out there who will appreciate you for who you are. You just have to find him. And if you just put yourself out there, I'm sure that he'll probably turn up pretty quickly.

Of course, everyone can improve themselves by eating better and exercising, but you have to realize that even after all that, you are still you. And you are good enough. And someone out there—probably more than one—thinks you are too. In spite of what you may think is wrong with you, someone else can find a zillion other things that are *right* you with you. This is why you should never tear yourself down in this way.

So the next time you find yourself putting yourself down, remember that you may be the only one doing this because someone else might think that you're pretty cool just the way you are. You are attractive and as long as you know this and are confident in yourself, everyone around you will be able to see it.

LOW SELF-ESTEEM

Do you know that one of the most common elements of almost all bad deeds? The one thread that runs through much of the wrong that people do to each other? It's that usually the perpetrator suffers from some form of low self-esteem. People go out and hurt each other or themselves because they feel that they are somehow not good enough for something better or that they want to bring down everyone around them so that they can feel good about themselves.

Yes, if there's one universal enemy of mankind as a whole, it is that of low self-esteem. As I briefly alluded to in the chapter regarding jealousy, this is the great underminer of many a great person. It limits potential and will weaken even the strongest of individuals. It breaks everybody down equally. However, it especially breaks down women.

Low self-esteem is a killer. Literally and figuratively. It will make you do things that you would never do otherwise. It will make you take abuse and cause you to lower your standards. It will make you expect less out of yourself. And the thing is, if you saw someone else doing some of the stuff that it compels you to do, you would think that the other person is a pretty pathetic person.

It's that powerful. It will make you chase after men and put up with behavior a normal person wouldn't. Some people aren't that affected by it, but many are. Those that aren't probably usually are very confident in themselves and don't take everything so personally. They realize that everything in the world is not directly related to them and therefore can shrug off most of the bad stuff that happens to them. It makes them not care because they know that most bad things that happen are either due to random circumstances or are the result of other people's actions. People with low self-esteem think that they're to blame for everything or that they deserve bad things because they're not good enough. They live at the center of a very self-centered universe. They can't not care because they think everything is somehow directly related to them!

Why it affects women more than men is anyone's guess. The reason is probably most rooted in the fact that most women are competitive and because of this many of them think that they are lesser than other people. Maybe it's because many girls are simply told from an early age that they are just not as good as the boys, that they aren't good at sports or math. As a result, it makes them think that they aren't good at other things as well. As I mentioned earlier, it could also just be a form of narcissism. Some people may think that everything in the world is some sort of indicator of their unworthiness, that everything is related to them in some way. I've certainly seen this aspect in many women. However, it's not true of all. Regardless of its cause, it is something that you must overcome if you are to be a sexy and confident woman.

How you do it is like this. Every time you feel that you aren't good enough or want to do something that you feel is beneath you just to keep some guy or job, take a step back and ask yourself why you think this. Is it because you're so low that you're not good enough for anything better? Is it because you really aren't good enough? Or is it because of some other issue that has nothing to do with the issue at hand. You need to realize why you do the things make you unhappy. Once you can do this, you can start building yourself up. You have to start neutralizing your low-self-esteem. You have to think that you are good enough and if you feel otherwise understand that there's probably no real reason why you feel this way.

You have to realize that low self-esteem is at the root of many of your problems. Once you do this, you will automatically start to overcome them. After that you can take steps to win back your feelings of confidence. Then you can become the confident woman you know yourself to be, despite what your low-self-esteem may tell you.

DESPERATION ISN'T SEXY

I know you've seen this girl. She's the one who sits around waiting for the guy she likes to call. And when he doesn't, she calls or starts texting him just to make sure that he didn't get her number wrong. Or she throws herself at him just to get him to notice her. Or she starts financing his motorcycle and offroading hobby. Or she has sex with him just to get him to go out again. Or even worse, she gets pregnant just to get him to stay.

She's desperate and she does everything in her power to let her man know it. Hopefully, you aren't her, but if you are, it's not over yet. There's always hope when it comes to improving yourself and your negative behaviors.

Desperation is a very pathetic state. Everybody has been there and everybody has been desperate about something. Whether it's a job or a man, everybody has wanted something so badly that they're willing to lower themselves to get it. That they're willing to make themselves look like asses just to get that shot. They get desperate. And the reason why they're desperate is because they believe deep down that whatever it is they want is unattainable. If it's a job, it's one that they're not going to get. If it's a man, they know that he doesn't like them. This is where the panic sets in and from there on in, it's desperation city. If the desperate person is lucky, they will be pushed aside and looked over. If they're not, the focus of their desperation will give them false hope, use them and then discard them. This leaves them feeling even worse about themselves than they would have felt before.

I know that this is easy for me to say, but you cannot be this way. You cannot be a sexy and confident woman if you're desperate about anything. Especially a man. If a man doesn't want you, then you don't want him. It's that simple. You're not going to convince him otherwise. Some men are like jackals and prey on desperate women. Especially those women of a certain age. They promise them love and families and babies and then drain them emotionally and sometimes financially. They prowl around until they find a weak woman and then pounce. After they're finished, they are merciless and think nothing of leaving a woman to question and doubt her self-worth for many years to follow.

You must be aware of yourself. You must be aware of how you're coming off in this world. A person of value is never desperate. People are desperate for them.

I know that everyone falls in love and that sometimes you can't help but make a fool out of yourself for someone. Everybody does this. This is okay. However, when that behavior crosses the line into cringing pathetic begging and whining then you're being desperate. For example have you ever called a man because you thought he may have written your number down wrong and this is the reason why he hasn't called you? Have you ever thought about getting pregnant just so your boyfriend won't break up with you? This is the kind of thing I'm talking about. These are big no-nos.

Never do anything with the sole intention of convincing a man to like you or go out with you. You can never try to make him be attracted to you. You must let him be attracted to you. Don't worry about this kind of thing. If you can just put yourself out there as a sexy and confident woman who doesn't care if a man is attracted to her or not, you will attract men. There is no doubt about it. If you are sexy and confident, when you attract men, you can have your pick. You'll also have more time to evaluate just who this is that's trying to gain your favor because it will be on your schedule. When you try to make them attracted to you, there's no telling what you're going to pull in.

Desperation is never sexy. Never be a desperate woman. If you are, you'll have only yourself to thank for your problems.

NEVER CHASE A MAN

Now that we've talked about desperation, we need to talk about a related subject. This is something that involves a role reversal and while desperation is not necessarily a key factor, it can certainly appear that way to a lot of outside observers. What I'm talking about is when a woman chases a man. If you're sexy and confident, this is something that should never happen.

One of the most uncomfortable things I have ever seen is when a woman chases a man. Not literally chase, mind you, but rather go after him as though he was the princess and she is the knight in shining armor. It just doesn't work. It puts a woman in a position that is very unflattering not only from a power standpoint, but also from an historical one as well. Did Cinderella chase after Prince Charming? Or Sleeping Beauty? Or Snow White? Did Josephine chase Napolean? I don't think so.

Now, I know what year it is. And I know that this sounds really old-fashioned, but a woman should never chase a man. Never. It puts her in a bad position because it makes her look needy and desperate whether she is or not and it also upsets the balance of power in a relationship. Sure, some men like aggressive women, but you need to keep it in check at first and let him do the chasing. At the beginning anyway, a woman should always be in the person who is asked out.

Of course, there are going to be times when you are going to be interested in a man and you want him to ask you out. This is normal. In this case, of course, you can flirt or talk to him and make yourself available. But you have to do this subtlety. Very subtlety. If he thinks you're too interested or too needy he's either going to be scared off or he's going to use you. You have present yourself in such a way to make him think that it's his idea to ask you out. Once again, you cannot chase him. But if he shows no interest whatsoever, he is not interested. Move on. Believe me, there will be other men who are interested in who you are and what you have to offer.

The thing is that when a woman chases a man, she puts herself in a position of being viewed as desperate whether she is or not. She may just be aggressive or really sure of herself. She may just know what she wants in a man and goes after it. I know this may be tough for some girls, but they need to hold back. For lack of a better way of putting it, she cannot allow herself to act like a man in these circumstances. Impressions are everything in the dating world. You have to make the correct one in the beginning or you're potentially setting yourself up for a bad relationship because the guy is going to get the idea that you want him too badly. When this happens, some men will see it as an opportunity to take advantage. This is because a woman who is considered by a man to be desperate will be used by that man. Either that, or she will be considered a joke. Not only by him and his friends but by other women. A sexy and confident woman never has to chase a man. She doesn't need to. A man who isn't interested enough in her to ask her out isn't even worth her time of day. It's all about confidence. Not everyone is going to love you or be attracted to you. You just have to be sure that you don't waste your time on these types. This means never chasing.

But what do you do if a man drops you? If he's the love of your life and he just dumps you like you're yesterday's garbage? Do you run after him and beg him to come back? No, you move on. Quickly. It may be tough but it's imperative that you forget him as soon as he's out the door. This lets him know that he was not in charge of the relationship and that he meant a lot less to you than you did to him. It will be difficult, especially if you love him, but this is the best way. You cannot ever let a man know that you're pining over him after a breakup. If you do this, it will not only boost his ego, but will also make him feel that he's better than he really is. You don't want him to feel good about breaking up with you. You want him to feel bad because when you act like you don't care when he leaves, he will know the big mistake he made. This is what you want. You want him to feel worse than you.

So whenever the urge strikes you and you feel that so-and-so is "The One" *if only he would just notice you*, stop and take stock of what you're doing. If you go after him like you're the man, he will just think you're foolish or will think there is some justification to his already over-inflated ego. Just take it cool and don't chase him. If he's interested, you'll know it. If not, you don't need him.

NEVER PUT YOURSELF BENEATH A MAN

As I mentioned before there are traditional roles for women when it comes to dating that must be adhered to. This is mainly in regards to the beginning of a relationship when a woman should allow the man do all the work. However, this is about as far as it goes. Gender roles are one thing, but how you're treated in the relationship is another. While a woman should be placed on a pedestal, this doesn't mean that her role in life is to clean it. Unless she wants to, of course.

You have to keep in mind that a sexy and confident woman stands on her own two feet. She may want companionship but she doesn't need it. She may want a man, but she doesn't need one. This means that she doesn't have to go out of her way to please a man. In other words, she never has to demean herself to get one. She doesn't have to lower herself. She doesn't have to be his maid or his mother. She is his partner in life and this is how the relationship should always be viewed. She should never be expected to do anything just because she is "the woman" of the relationship. If a man thinks that the fact that a woman is female makes her lower than him, then maybe the woman should rethink the relationship.

A sexy and confident woman only does things she wants to do regarding a man. If she wants to cook for him, great. But if she cooks for him because he expects her to do it because she's a woman, then this is wrong. The same thing goes for everything else in the relationship, including sex. If she wants to do it then it's fine. But if it's just because she's expected to because she's a woman, then it's wrong.

Now before we go any further, please know that I'm not a person who thinks that men are evil and that women should act like they are. My issue is that there are men who think that because these roles are generally considered more feminine that this gives them an excuse not to do them. Or that that they are beneath him. This is so horribly wrong on so many levels. I guess one could say that my problem is not so much with what women do for men, it's why they do these things. Do they do them because they want to do nice things for their men and families? Or do they do them because the man thinks he's above such things?

A woman should always know that she has options. And that if a man is expecting her to do things because he's her "superior" then she should know that she can always tell him to take a walk. There are other men out there who will treat her better. She should always know this. And he should too, if he's smart.

OTHER WOMEN? DON'T LET THEM BEAT YOU DOWN

Are you the type of person who hates to work with a bunch of other women? Do you hate the cattiness? Do you hate the two-facedness and talking behind the back that so many women seem to do to each other?

Well, you're not alone. You probably wouldn't like this kind of environment unless you're the one doing the talking and being catty. And if this isn't you, then you're probably the subject of the talking and cattiness.

As I keep saying, women are their own worst enemies. It's almost laughable if it wasn't so true and so unnecessary. Not only do they sabotage themselves, but they also sabotage each other. Many of them take every opportunity they can find to tear each other down and diminish any accomplishments that other women make. When they think that somebody is rising above them, the claws come out. And if a man is involved, watch out! There's no telling what lengths they might stoop to. Rather than looking at being a woman as a sisterhood and rejoicing in the triumphs of other women, they become jealous and feel like they need to bring the offending/succeeding woman down.

But as I said, this is so unneccesary and only serves to keep you in a negative position. If you can avoid doing this and rise above when it's done to you, you will be much happier in life and will be a much more successful person.

I don't know what it is, but women seem to be taught from an early age to compete with each other and to tear each other down. All it takes is for another woman to become successsful or to lose weight or to try to fix herself up and the remarks will start. This is entirely counterproductive. The thing is that if you can build each other up, then everyone will succeed. Men and other women depend on women fighting amongst themselves. Unscupulous bosses and players will use it to get what they want.

If you want an easy-to-relate-to example of this kind of behavior, just watch any reality show. What inevitably happens every time someone tries to start an all girl alliance? You guessed it. It falls apart. Sure, everyone starts out with good intentions, but all it takes is for one man to come in and start manipulating and the women turn against each other and subsequently get defeated. It happens so much that it's almost not even worth remarking about. However, it is a good indicator of how the real world works. If women would just get together and stop trashing each other, they could take over the world. They're the ones who have the babies. They're the ones who have what men want. They're the ones who should be doing the manipulating, but instead they are the ones who get manipulated.

Like many of the other ills that women and girls suffer, this one is yet again caused by low self-esteem and jealousy. If you weren't threatened by the fact that another woman is doing something for herself, you would be happy. For some reason, many women take it as a personal attack when another woman does well. This is completely ludicrous and only makes them seem like very small people. As I've mentioned before, a good example of this happens in offices where most of the women are middle-aged. Have you noticed how vicious they become when a younger woman begins working there? They begin to stoop to high-school tactics like bullying and berating just to make the younger woman feel badly about herself. And this is purely due to jealousy. And most of the time, there is absolutely nothing to be gained by this kind of behavior. Does getting the younger woman to quit make anyone feel better about themselves? Of course this is a specific example, but this kind of thing carries over to most other situations where women are around each other. It's a very unfortunate thing but it happens all the time.

So the next time you feel like you're being torn down by another woman, don't take it personally. Realize that it's not you, it's her. Take the high road and realize that this woman is just falling prey to one of the oldest pitfalls in the book. Also realize that you're probably doing something right if she is so adamant about tearing you down. In other words, she already thinks she's on the bottom and is just trying to bring you down to it too. Don't let her. And if you're the one doing the tearing down, realize that this is the time to stop it.

HOW MEN OPERATE

To capture the beast, you have to become the beast.

Well, this may be true when it comes to hunting, but when it comes to dating this is not a good idea. However, it is a good idea to know how your quarry operates and thinks. In other words, you have to know how men operate.

Yes, if you want to be the girl that men want, then you have to know how men operate. This means that you have to understand how they think if you want to know what they want.

This is pretty easy. They want you. This is how men operate. Good men that is. Good, decent men want a woman who accepts them for them. Good or bad. And to do this, you just have to be honest about who you are. If you are not honest, it will eventually come out. Most men are just looking for a woman who likes them and wants to be with them. They want a woman who doesn't make them feel badly about themselves. They want a woman who doesn't hound them about the little things. They want one who makes them feel good about themselves. In this sense, they want the same thing as you, to be wanted.

Of course, as with everything there are exceptions. Usually these are the players and the men who think they are God's gifts. But you don't need these types. Besides they aren't worth it. Do you really want to compete with a man for mirror time?

One thing to realize is that good men usually are much more straightforward than women in how they operate. They don't really beat around the bush that much and try to play guessing games. Sure, like women, some of them may have rejection and self-image issues, but they are usually less complicated than this. Some men may be shy but most are easy reads. You can tell when they like a girl. And many, unless they are players of course, will probably not play with your emotions that much. Especially when they are really interested. Even though they play it cool, you can still tell. Regardless, let them make the effort to get things started.

But the bottom line is that when they like you, they like the real you. And to be the real you, you have to be yourself. You cannot be someone else. You cannot fake it. You cannot cater to their needs. You cannot lower yourself for them and you cannot put yourself in a subordinate position. Of course there are going to be some men that will want you do to this. This is another aspect of knowing how men operate. These are the men who are only out to use you. These are the men you need to avoid. The thing to realize is that if a man is really making you work to get his affections, if he is playing games and playing hard to get, this is probably a red flag that this man is either not ready for a relationship or he is just out to use you.

Also, here's a little tip for you insecure girls out there who always need to be reassured that your man actually wants to be with you. Don't ever test a man. You know what I mean here. Don't ever dream up these challenges that a man must pass in order to prove his affection. For example, don't ever chew a man out and then run from the room and then see if he follows you in order to test to see if he truly is in love with you. This will not work and you will be disappointed. The reason for this is not because he isn't in love with you, but rather because men don't think like this.

They are usually too obvious-minded in this regard. If you get mad at them, they don't see it as a test. They see it as anger and usually won't want to be around you. Men are very simple-minded and direct when it comes to human interaction so don't test them. This is very unfair to them and it's also just a very immature thing to do.

Men who are good and decent will not want you to be beneath them. Sure, some of them may be old-fashioned about gender roles, but these types are easily differentiated from the creeps who just want to use you. It's in their intention. Intention is everything in relationships.

Understanding how men operate is easy. Most are just looking for approval and genuine relationships. Some may be a little more awkward than others, but essentially most are just like women in what they want and less complicated in how they operate.

DEALING WITH PLAYERS

If there's anything that can tear a good girl down faster than anything, it's dealing with a player. These guys are horrible. In fact, I hate even using the term *player* but feel compelled to in order to convey just who exactly I'm talking about.

When I mean that they'll break a good girl down, I mean exactly that. Through their game playing and manipulation, they'll make a confident girl start to doubt herself. She'll question her looks as well as her intentions. If she falls too hard for one of these fools, she'll end up with a broken heart and a lot of doubt. And probably a little desperation about having lost the guy. He will make her turn pathetic and will rejoice in the fact that he has turned her into a fool. To him, he is just another conquest and nothing more. Except maybe a future booty-call.

The thing you need to keep in mind when dealing with players is to not deal with them at all. If you can establish some good ground rules for how you date, you'll be able to sidestep these losers. You can start by not playing games. Especially when they're put out there by these guys. Also never chase a man. No man is worth it. Any man worth having will chase you. Of course, these rules are up to you, but you need to keep in mind that you should never do anything that you're not comfortable with. That includes calling a man. Or putting up with him when he doesn't call you back for weeks at a time. Or when he wants to make you his booty call. Remember, you're a hot commodity. Don't let some man treat you badly just because he thinks he can.

The biggest thing is keeping your self-respect and if you meet a guy who wants to make you compromise your standards, then run the other way. A sexy and confident woman doesn't have to play games because she's above them. Most of these players will be scared of her anyway because they know all too well how little tolerance she has of their nonsense. She is nobody's booty call and does not play games. She's sure of herself and doesn't let low self-esteem dictate her choice of dating.

The hardest thing about dealing with players is that they usually know how to work women. They play on their weaknesses. They know that women like to be complimented and that they like little presents. They will turn these things against women and then after they get what they want, they'll leave. Then, she might become a booty call to him. This is something that he knows she'll gladly do just for the opportunity to get to see him again and maybe get a relationship going. They will give a woman everything but what she really wants, his love. The thing is that they can really make a woman feel good about herself. That is, is until they're finished with her.

I know that many girls consider themselves players as well. I think this is also a bad thing and is once again usually indicative of low self-esteem. Why else would a girl want to play games? Why else would she want to be a bed-post notcher? And many of them think that they can outplay the male players. Usually they're wrong because most men who are players do not suffer from low self-esteem, but rather an over inflated ego. They don't have the same weaknesses and will ultimately use a girl's self-doubt against her.

If you're going to be sexy and confident, you cannot waste time with players. They aren't worth your time because any game that they might be playing isn't worth the effort. Find a decent guy who respects you and you'll find that while his game may be a little different, it will be much more rewarding because more than likely, it will be real and not just some complicated way of getting into your pants.

STOP LOSING YOUR SELF-RESPECT

While some women have suffered with low self-esteem throughout all their lives, many of them don't start out in life insecure. They start out strong and confident. But this is before they start dating and going into the work place. This is when they start being beaten down by men and by co-workers. They also become beaten down by life. As a result of this, many times, they start feeling badly about themselves because they start doing things that they otherwise would not have done if they hadn't been broken down so badly. They start to do things in order to feel good about themselves and to get others to feel good about them that they would have never dreamed they would have ever done. They begin to make mistakes. From this, it all goes downhill and eventually, they lose respect for themselves.

For many women, the key to being confident and feeling good about themselves entails them not losing their self-respect. To achieve this ideally means that they never do things that they regret or ever make a mistake. Well, I've got news for you. People make mistakes. They do things they regret. However, you can only lose your self-respect when you keep making the same mistakes over and over again when you know full well that you can do better.

Yes, you know what I'm talking about.

Do you hate yourself when you have a one-night stand? But do you keep having them? Well, this is what I'm talking about. When you make a mistake, it's okay to feel bad about it. However, don't keep putting yourself in a situation where you keep feeling bad about it. Stop the behavior. Do you feel bad when you are mean to others? Stop being mean! This is the answer.

The great thing about self-respect is that it can be regained. Remember what I was saying about your past meaning nothing? It's true. Each day is truly a new day. Each day presents many opportunities to do better. You can improve yourself if you just stop making the same mistakes that are holding you back.

You've only lost your self-respect when you fail to do better when you know that you can do better. You can always do better. If you know you're doing something that is beneath your standards, just stop doing it. It may be a little tough at first, but just think at how good you'll feel once you've overcome it.

FIXER-UPPERS? PROS AND CONS

Are you the type of person who always sees the diamond in the rough? Are you the one that looks for the silver lining in every cloud? Do you see the prince behind every frog? If so, then great. It's good that there's optimistic and positive people like you in this world. However, you should only let this optimism go so far. It's one thing to see beyond the bad things about a person, it's another thing to try to change them. Or to date a person with the intention of doing this.

There's always room for improvement. Everyone can make changes that will make them better people. However, a person can only do so much. And they have to do it for themselves. This is why most women should think twice about a fixer-upper. You should really evaluate just what you're in for. If it's just his wardrobe that needs fixed, than that's no problem. It it's his hygiene, then that's no problem either. However, if he has serious issues then maybe you should reconsider. No, I'm not saying that you should be an elitist. You should give people a fair shot. But if there's not that much there to begin with, then maybe you should scrap him and start from scratch.

As with anything, there are different layers and break-even points when it comes to fixer-uppers. As I mentioned earlier, if he dresses badly, then you can fix that. If he lacks self-confidence, that can be fixed too (but watch out that you don't create an egotistical monster!) but if he's abusive, a drug user or is just a mean person, then it's going to take more than the love of a woman to fix this guy. He needs professional help and you will only bring yourself down and ruin your self-esteem and confidence if you try to help him. This is because most likely you will fail.

The thing about fixer-uppers is that you can only fix the outside package. There has to be something there to begin with. It's just like remodeling a house. If it doesn't have good bones, then it's probably a complete tear-down situation. When this happens, the remodeler has to ask himself, is it worth it to remodel or just start fresh? You should take this same outlook when it comes to dating fixer-uppers. Is it worth it? Is it accomplishable? You can't be Don Quixote in these situations. You have to be realistic; otherwise you will waste a lot of time, money and self-esteem on a loser.

Survival is the name of the game when it comes to being human. Especially when you're a woman. If a man is merely in need of a polish, then go for it. But if he's a complete overhaul, then maybe you need to leave him for someone who can really help him. Like a psychiatrist.

A PARTICULAR MAN TO AVOID

Have you ever wondered why some men never seem to find anyone with whom to share their lives? Have you ever wondered why some men are alone? They seem kind of normal, so what's going on with them? Maybe they're just unlucky in love, you think. Or maybe they just missed the boat. Sadly however, usually it's neither of these. They're not alone because they've been overlooked by love. They're alone because they're defective in some way.

These are the men you need to avoid.

Now there are some good men out there. Many good men. Men who you want to bring home to meet the parents and that you want to spend your life with. But there are some really bad ones too. These are men that you want to avoid like the plague. If you don't, they will either waste your time or possibly even hurt you. Mentally and physically.

Of course, there are the usual types that many of these books bring up. You know, the toxic bachelors, the Peter Pans, the bad boys and the Mama's boys. These are the types that will waste your time and money. I think we've touched on these already when we discussed bad choices in men. Also, I think that these types have been discussed to death in other books. What I want to address is the other types, the real bad dudes. The creeps. These are the type that you must avoid if you are to remain safe and sane. The types I'm talking about are the potential stalkers. The ones who, if you decide that you don't want to go out anymore, will start showing up where you work and will start harrassing you on the phone. These are the types that will hurt you. The bad thing about it is that many of these men seem completely normal on the outside. Quiet and polite. And boring. The type of man that a girl wouldn't mind bringing home to her family. However, if she does do this to one of these guys, she runs the risk of never being able to get away from him.

So how can you tell these types? As you probably realize it can be a little difficult because the hide themselves well. That is until they feel slighted. However, I have noticed one major common denominator. *They have usually never been in a meaningful relationship.* That's right. They have never been in a relationship. Now you younger girls out there, I'm not talking about your nineteen-year-old boyfriend here. He just hasn't had the time. The ones I'm talking about are the middle-aged men. The ones who are in their late twenties and thirties (and beyond) and have never been married, lived with a woman or had a girlfriend. Or they say they have never been in love. If you happen across a man like this, run! Stop it before it gets started. These guys are single for a reason. They are the leftovers. They are the castoffs. They don't know how to act in a relationship and it's not your job to teach them. There is a reason why they're still alone. They are damaged goods. They are meant to be single. The term *natural selection* should come to mind here. Sure, there might be some chance that a guy like this is normal, but not likely. More often than not, they're stunted and if you give them the time of day, you'll become the object of their affections whether you like it or not. And this is not a good thing, believe me.

Also if a man is extremely against single moms, especially if he's middle-aged, it's also a good sign that there is something wrong with him. Either he thinks he's God's gift and can pick and choose as he pleases or he wants you all to himself—not necessarily a good thing. If you have kids, he will treat them badly. He's warning you what he's about without even knowing he's doing it. You just have to read the signs.

However, as I said earlier, if the guy is younger and actually has a good excuse as to why he's never been in a real relationship, then the ball is in your court. Maybe he's been in the army. Maybe he's been in the Peace Corps. This is still pretty weak, but since he's younger and hasn't had time for as many experiences, it might be okay to cut him some slack. But if he's over twenty-eight or so, avoid, avoid, avoid! Or if you're absolutely smitten, proceed with caution. Ask questions and try to get a line of why he's never had a relationship before you get too deeply in.

So if you want a major warning sign about a man who you should avoid, just remember this: If he's middle-aged and hasn't ever had a real relationship, run. Don't be his first. Because if you stay around and he gets upset at you, he might just be your last.

MAKE THEM RESPECT YOU

Women have to put up with a lot. They're the ones who have to endure pregnancy. They're the ones who raise the children. And they have to do so much more to get ready to go out in the morning. So with this in mind, do they really need the added burden of having to put up with a man's disrepect?

People say that you have to earn respect. I believe this is true, but when it comes to women and dating, sometimes it takes a little more than this. If a man isn't decent, you will have to make him respect you. You will have to demand that he treat you well. This is what a confident woman does.

Yes, you have to make him.

In case you have no idea what I'm talking about, does your man routinely call you a bitch? Does he stand you up? Does he go for days without calling you? Does he treat you indifferently? These are just a few examples, but if he's doing this, he's disrepecting you. He's treating you like crap and he expects you to like it. Or at least to excuse it because after all, he's "just a man." This is so wrong. If this kind of thing happens to you on a regular basis, you need to start standing up for yourself. You need to make him start respecting you or he needs to hit the road.

Just as when we discussed how you should expect men to treat you like a lady, most of this has to do with expectations. If you don't expect a man to treat you well, then you won't be treated well. You need to remember that you're worth it and you deserve to be treated with respect. If you expect less, then you will get less. This is just the way it is. I'm not saying that you should go so far with this and dump the guy if he doesn't bring you diamond earrings everytime you meet, but he should at least act like he's glad to see you.

I know that it's going to be hard to assert yourself at first, but you will have to try. And the more you do it the easier it will get. It's fairly simple to do it, too. When he does something disrespectful to you, let him know about it. Tell him how you feel. Be cool, calm and collected and don't yell. Never scream or act irrational no matter how tempting this may be. Just make your point. Make sure there are consequences and follow up on them. Eventually, he'll learn. Or you'll learn that he's just a disrepectful man who's not worth the effort. And if the situation is so scary that you're afraid to say anything to this man, maybe you need to think about getting out of the relationship. Normal people in normal relationships don't scare each other.

One thing that you may want to take into account is that your man may have never been taught how to treat a woman. He may have grown up thinking that disrespect towards the female is just a way of life. You need to try to figure out if this is the case or is he just a jerk. If he just needs a little retraining, then go for it. If he loves you, then this shouldn't be that big of a deal. Just let him know how you feel when he does something that hurts you. If he's a good one, he'll make an effort towards change. However, if he's resistant and refuses to reform, or even goes out of his way to disrespect you even further, you may want to reconsider the relationship.

Disrespect happens in many places. It can happen in your relationship, at the office or just in dealing with other people. The people who are disprecting you could even be other women. Regardless, stand up for yourself. Sure, they may jump back at you, but you have to be prepared. You are a person who deserves respect. You should never be made to feel less than just because someone else thinks that it's their privilege to do so. Most people when you confront them in a cool and calm way without yelling or screaming will get your point and improve their behavior. Especially if they want to please you. If they don't, well, they aren't worth the effort. But never take their crap.

YOU'RE NOT A TEENAGER ANYMORE

Being a teenager can be tough. There is so much going on with your body and mind that the momentum you were building up as a person when you were prepubescent just goes out the window when you hit puberty. It causes a lot of insecurity and sometimes this can affect you for a long time even after you've passed the teenage years. This is why it's important that you realize, after you decide that you are going to be sexier and more confident woman, you are no longer a teenager.

Of course, I know that you know that you're no longer a teenager. However, I think that you need to realize, in your mind, that you really need to grow into yourself and get over the insecurities you had when you were a teenager. I know that this is when many women's problems with themselves and their self-images form because everything is new and their bodies are changing. This happens with boys too. It's like when you're a child, everything is okay and you think that when you're an adult things are going to be a certain way. However, then puberty hits and you're like, whoa! Is this the way it really is? It's nowhere near what you expected. You're not the gorgeous supermodel you always suspected you would be when you grew up. Instead you're this awkward, more hormonal version of yourself! I think it really causes a lot of self-doubt in people because the high school years are when many people's self-images are formed. Sure, when they go to college and beyond they may outgrow some of these issues, but just see what happens when they go back to this environment. It's the same thing all over again. I know it will be tough, but you have to overcome this time if you are to be *the you* that you know yourself to be.

I think that many of these insecurities you have over being awkward and rejected carry over into adulthood. They grow and mutate into other issues but the end result is that they keep you from becoming the woman that you want to be. If you'll notice, the girls who were very confident in high school are usually still quite confident as adults and the girls who weren't are still not. This is exactly what I'm talking about.

The thing you have to do is just realize that this was an awkward time for everyone. Even the cool kids. You were just not as aware of their issues as you were yours. You amplified your flaws and your problems and minimized theirs. Everyone has an awkward time. You just have to realize that yours has past.

If you don't believe me when I tell you this stuff, just take a look at yourself in the mirror. What are your flaws? I'll bet they are the same things you thought about yourself back when you were a teenager. Even if you've lost a lot of weight since then, I'll still bet you think you're fat. Right? You have to realize that you were looking at yourself with a flawed perspective back then. You had no life experience and had no real idea of what was beautiful. And you definitely didn't know what men like in a woman. In case you still don't, here's a clue. They like everything!

Just remember that you are an adult now and those awkward teenage, high school years are over. You're a grown woman and not an awkward girl. You have power and the sooner you realize that you have outgrown this old image you created for yourself back then, the sooner you will be come into your own. And if you are still a teenage girl, then realize that this time will past. Just don't stay in this place in your mind. Things will get better.

YOU'RE READY

Well, we're at the end.

Are you ready to be a sexy and confident dreamgirl yet? I suspect that you were before you read this book. You already knew that you were the type of girl that men wanted but you just didn't know how to pull it off. Or you knew that you were the type of girl that men wanted, but didn't like the kind of men who wanted you. But now you've got that all squared away and are ready to go full force into life with the sexy and confident you.

Everyone has insecurities. This is not the issue. It's how you deal with them that's important. You can either keep letting them hinder you or you can make positive changes to overcome them.

Sexy and confident is the way to be when you're a woman these days. Gone are the days of the frumpy feminazi and the "one of the guys" strong business woman. The world is ready for a strong and feminine woman who knows what she wants and isn't afraid to go out and get it. She knows that her femininity is an asset to be used rather than a liability to be hidden.

Women are powerful and when you're sexy and confident, you're using this power to its full extent. You know that this is the stuff that dreamgirls are made of. You also know that a man who isn't ready for this isn't ready for her and is able to move on to someone better.

I trust that you've learned that you are a very important person who deserves to treated well. You deserve respect and you shouldn't have to take any abuse from anyone. You deserve good relationships and treatment from men. You also deserve to be treated with respect by your co-workers. If you don't, I know that you will speak up for yourself and let your displeasure be heard. This is what confidence is. It's being able to expect the best out of yourself and to be treated well by those around you. It also means that you don't have to make others look bad in order to make yourself look good. You know that when you bring out the best in others, it also brings out the best in you.

I hope that this book has brought you closer to becoming a more self-confident woman. I hope that's it's shown you that being a woman is great and that when you're sexy and confident you're not only being true to yourself, but you're also being the best that you can be. I also hope that you've learned that when you're the best you can be, you truly are a dreamgirl.

The world is yours. You just have to know it.

Hopefully, now you do.

CPSIA information can be obtained at www.ICGtesting.com
Printed in the USA
BVOW082205150812

297924BV00001B/51/P